AF563397

Mayakovsky
Maximum Access

selected poems by Vladimir Mayakovsky
translated by Jenny Wade

SENSITIVE SKIN BOOKS

MAYAKOVSKY MAXIMUM ACCESS

Book Design: Bernard Meisler
Book Cover Illustration and Design: Leslie Hardie

Published in the United States by **Sensitive Skin Books**.
Mill Valley, CA

First Edition 2018 **Sensitive Skin Books**
www.sensitiveskinmagazine.com
www.facebook.com/sensitiveskin

Library of Congress Control Number: 2018935661

ISBN: 978-0-9961570-7-0

To all the fools who abandoned "shameful good sense" and fell in love with Russian poetry.

Contents

Author's Preface

My first encounter with Mayakovsky was humiliating. As an intermediate Russian student I tried to hack my way through "Backbone flute," but was quickly overwhelmed by the convoluted language, the strange and insistent use of the instrumental case, and the multitude of words which failed to appear in any dictionary. Then there were the elusive cultural, historical and literary references (Where or what is Strelka? Or Sokolniki? Who goes extinct on a mountain crag? Why is the word "god" in lower case? Why are crowds crawling out of trenches?) To top it off, I couldn't even scan it—the meter was irregular and completely unpredictable.

But I felt compelled to keep grinding away. Hearing the poem recited—the rhythm, the sound and the sweep of it—gave me chills, it made me want to start weeping. It struck me like an unholy marriage between Beethoven's 3rd Symphony and Iggy Pop's "Raw Power." It gave me an inkling of why my Soviet friends hung portraits not of family members, but of poets, on their walls; of what inspired them to memorize thousands of lines of verse; of why crowds gathered at Mayakovsky's monument in Moscow, even in the face of intense official disapproval, to hear and recite poetry.

What I wanted was a gentle hand to guide me through the poem—a single source with the stress marks, an explanation of context, and a translation that eased me into the Russian itself. And not just for "Flute," I needed help with lots of Mayakovsky poems. But I was never able to find the guide I envisioned, and it eventually dawned on me that I should create it myself.

This book was a group effort. It would have been impossible to write without two key people: my friend Natasha Ziltsova, a retired Soviet engineer and poetry lover, who met with me every week to go over stress marks and initial impressions, and the incomparable Professor Anna Muza from UC Berkeley, who patiently reviewed every translation, answered all of my questions, and offered a multitude of insightful comments, suggestions and corrections. Much of the commentary in this book came directly from our discussions. I'm also grateful to the editors and proof-readers of the book: Anton Yakovlev, Pamela Pierce, Justine Frischmann, Bernard Meisler, and Luciann Meisler. Thanks to everyone!

A hurricane, fire, water, a roar

In the fall of 1912, 19-year-old Vladimir Mayakovsky hit the Russian art scene like a tornado. Debuting with the notorious manifesto *A Slap in the Face of Public Taste*, M and his Futurist friends created one uproar after another with their performances in the theaters, cafes and streets of Moscow and Petersburg. By the end of 1913, in addition to antagonizing the public with speeches on topics such as "Egyptians and Greeks, who stroked dry black cats," and "Folds of fat in arm-chairs," M had published his first collection of poems (entitled *Me!*); had written, directed and starred in his first play, *Vladimir Mayakovsky, A Tragedy*; and embarked upon a 17-city lecture and reading tour, during which he began work on one of the most ground-breaking poems of the era: "A cloud in trousers." In no time at all he had become one of the most famous and controversial players in the Russian literary world—"the hooligan in the yellow blouse."(1)

Tremendously energetic, he turned seamlessly from one art form to another for the next 20 years. He illustrated books. He exhibited canvases alongside Kandinsky, Malevich and Chagall. He designed theater sets, posters and costumes. He created hundreds of agitprop posters. He wrote essays on theater and literature. He wrote plays. He wrote screenplays. He starred in three films. He created ads for cigarettes, galoshes, cookies, pacifiers, and sausages. He wrote children's books. He edited the avant-garde journals *LEF* and *New LEF*, and thus, in addition to Futurism, helped usher in a second major art movement: Constructivism. He gave countless readings in clubs, theaters and, after the 1917 revolution, in factories, workers' clubs and Komsomol meetings. He traveled to Europe, Mexico and America as a journalist and cultural representative of the Soviet Union. Over the course of his career, he collaborated with the greatest Russian artists of the time, including Rodchenko, Meyerhold, Shostakovich, and Eisenstein.

And he wrote poetry—love poetry, death poetry, odes to the revolution, poems dedicated to the army, to Lenin, to the Brooklyn Bridge, to street signs, to the Atlantic Ocean, to tax collectors, and to his own "Beloved self." He invites the sun over for tea, he takes Napoleon for a walk on a leash, he offers Pushkin an editorial position at *LEF*. He's a hooligan, a fop strutting down Nevsky Prospect. He's a blasphemer, a savior, a sacrificial bull. He pivots from being a weepy violin to champion of the revolution, from a wide-eyed tourist a homesick traveler, from a zoo-keeper to a broken-hearted bear floating down the Neva on a block of ice. He grows claws,

---

(1) N. Serebrov. "О Маяковском." V. Maiakovskii v vospominaniiakh sovremenikov. Moscow, 1963. Maksim Moshkow and the Federal Agency of Print and Mass Communication. http://az.lib.ru/m/majakowskij_w_w/text_0120.shtml (accessed August 10, 2017). This was how M was characterized by the press, and the phrase became an epithet.

horns, fangs, feathers and tails. He heaps insults upon the petite bourgeoisie, upon his fellow poets, and upon God Almighty ("Why don't you just run along back to heaven where you belong?").

In the few months before his suicide in April, 1930, he wrote his last major poem, "At the Top of My Voice." He also performed at the Bolshoi Theater (reading from "Vladimir Ilyich Lenin"), premiered his play *The Bathhouse*, and produced the massive spectacle *Moscow is Burning*—a circus act with clowns, trapeze artists, parades, a stilt-walker, and trained animals. In addition to all of this, he somehow found the time and energy to organize a retrospective of his life's work.(2) At the opening, he turned to a friend and asked, "Did I do enough?"(3)

Russia has no shortage of great poets, but none of them rivets the attention like Mayakovsky. His dynamism and versatility make him unique. His interchanging and kaleidoscopic roles as dramatist, performer, graphic artist, propagandist and ad-man are all facets of Mayakovsky the poet. They contribute synergistically to his poetry, and are inseparable from his poetry. The dramatic use of persona, the declamatory rhythms and wit and snap of his rhymes, the vivid imagery and novel layout of text, the honed delivery of social commands, the mastery of branding and packaging—all engage the reader on multiple levels, and, coming together, deliver a exceptionally powerful poetic punch.

A defining quality of M's work is the startling and powerful use of persona. He typically assumes the starring role in his poems, and even when no "I" is present, it's clear who the speaker is. (He can't even resist appearing in his children's books—the narrator is "Uncle Mayakovsky"). His poems are about the drama of Mayakovsky: Mayakovsky, the hooligan-poet; Mayakovsky, the impassioned lover; Mayakovsky, the poet of the revolution; Mayakovsky, the misunderstood genius. And the drama is compelling, partly because of the repulsiveness of his character. The truth is, Mayakovsky often seems like a real jerk. His rallying cries on behalf of the state, his casual cruelty, his self-obsession, egotism and immaturity, his scorn for wholesale categories of fellow humans (fat people, educated people, the bourgeoisie, NEPmen, kulaks, bureaucrats, foreigners, the religious, not to mention contemporary writers and critics), his adolescent glee in shocking and aggravating the reader, his insistence on making a show of the grotesque—it's enough to make you turn away in disgust. But, at the same time, you're enthralled by the inventiveness and vitality of his language, his vivid imagery, and his absurd sense of humor. And what's more, you start to feel sorry for him. He's vulnerable, desperate to be loved, and completely willing to make a fool of himself. He's not afraid of being pathetic, hysterical and out of control, a clown. He lurches between grandiosity and ridiculousness, between the

(2) The exhibit was *20 Years' Work,* which opened Feb. 1 at the Writers' Club in Moscow. The Writers' Club was also where Mayakosvky's body was laid in state after his suicide.

(3) Victor Shklovsky, *Mayakovsky and his Circle,* trans. by Lily Feiler (The Cornwall Press, Inc., 1972), 198.

sublime and the horrific, and captivates with his readiness, at any point, to throw himself headlong over a cliff.

He was a masterful performer—tall, dramatically good-looking, with a dark charismatic presence and the timing and quick wittedness of a stand-up comic. As Elsa Troilet, a writer who knew him well, reported:

> "I've only ever seen one man—Mayakovsky—who could totally 'possess' a room. He played with the audience, teased it, taunted it like a mad bull and could always make it go the direction he wanted. God help any spectators who were stupid enough to confront him—they soon found themselves flattened on the tiles, knocked out by his arrogance, his casual manner and haughty humor." (4)

He used performing abilities to maximum effect in his poetry. But his greatest weapon was his voice:

> ". . . the audience . . . would find themselves absolutely overwhelmed by his orator's voice, his preacher's poems, reverberating with the strength and volume of a cathedral organ . . ."
>
> "The verses were made to be bellowed out. At hundreds of readings all over the Soviet Union he showed how his poetry should be declaimed. Everyone who heard him started imitating his delivery, reciting his poems to others, and they in turn did the same. That's how his work, the way to interpret it, was distributed orally. . . and still is today. Mayakovsky's work spread like wild fire through the USSR." (5)

The unique and revolutionary sound of Mayakovsky's verse—the declamatory rhythms, the dramatic intonation and emphatic delivery—was created for and honed by live performance.

Just as persona, performance and voice are major components of his poetry, so is design. The impact of Mayakovsky's visual arts training is clear not only in the intense imagery of his poetry, but in its layout and packaging. The prime example is the virtuosic poem "About That," where the dreamlike (and nightmarish) transmutation, flow and jumble of objects is matched by both the typography (a combination of *stolbik* and *lensenka*; more on this later) and the accompanying photomontages by Rodchenko. Among the patchwork of telephones, icy rivers and bridges, family

---

(4) Elsa Triolet, *Mayakovsky: A Memoir,* trans. by Susan de Muth (Hearing Eye, 2002), 29.

(5) Troilet, 24.

silverware, cannons, towers, and zoo animals are the repeated and prominent cutouts of Mayakovsky and his lover Lilya Brik. This is not just a synthesis of art forms, it's a masterpiece of branding—it's poetry literally created in the author's own image.

Mayakovsky's appeal to a contemporary western audience is not surprising: from a certain perspective, he looks more like an American rock star than a Russian Silver Age poet. The packed and rowdy performances, the embrace of mass (and multi) media, the cultivation of image, the promotional gimmicks, the mix of controversy and collossal popularity are, overall, more characteristic of Elvis than of M's literary peers.

And, like a proper rock star, Mayakovsky was an iconoclast. When *A Slap* was published, the dominant players on Russia's literary scene were the Symbolists. For over a decade, poets like Alexander Blok, Valery Bryusov and Konstantine Balmont had been producing refined and elegant work inspired by the beautiful worlds they envisioned beyond the physical plane—worlds they believed to be accessible only to the artist. Divorced from the social and political, they aspired towards the occult, the esoteric and the exotic. They presumed the role of high priests, seeking to reveal the transcendent through their poetry in a fusion of art, religion, and depravity. Next to these sophisticates, it's not surprising that Mayakovsky impressed people as an uncouth hooligan. Gumilyov compared the Futurists to hyenas. It's not so different than Frank Sinatra's reaction to Elvis in 1957: "Rock and roll . . . is sung and written for the most part by cretinous goons… it manages to be the martial music of every side-burned delinquent on the face of the earth . . . the most brutal, ugly, desperate, vicious form of expression it has been my misfortune to hear."

M may have seemed like a wild beast, but in truth he was ushering in a whole new poetic paradigm. Rejecting classicism, romanticism and mysticism, he embraced the urban—the gritty life and popular culture of the city streets. He crammed his work with images of city machinery, buildings and inhabitants, and with topical references to newspaper stories, popular novels, songs, dances (the mazurka, the kickapoo, and the two-step), and even advertisements. He was determined to drag art by force into the real world, into the machine age, into the here and now. Nothing was sacred—not God, not Pushkin, not the Symbolists, and especially not the values and conventions of bourgeois society. The notion of "art for art's sake," particularly for post-revolutionary Mayakovsky, was anathema. Poetry was a tool for shaping society, and the poet was not some passive instrument of the muse, but an active and crucial player on the national stage. While his contemporaries were acutely conscious of the Russian poetic tradition, M made a show of having zero respect for his predecessors, and brazenly forged his own way in poetic rhyme, rhythm and format. In content, philosophy and technique, Mayakovsky was, and still is, a poet of the modern era. In spite of Mayakovsky's rock-star appeal, much of his poetry remains stubbornly inaccessible to non-Russian speakers. There are wonderful translations available (many are listed in the bibliography), but no translation on its own can provide the full effect of the original poem: you can honor the structure by following the meter and rhyme scheme, but sacrifice meaning; you can honor the meaning, and sacrifice structure; or you can honor the tone by trying to recreate the poem in your own voice, and sacrifice the context. No matter what, you've failed. Translating Mayakovsky is an especially hopeless task. It might be impossible to express just how radical, how inventive and how funny he was—"the way he cut words short, his concise style, the innovative structure of his sentences, the creation of totally new words." To quote Troilet once more, "My generation needed an earthquake and that earthquake was Mayakovsky."[(6)] How do you translate an earthquake?

In this book, my translation strategy is to bring the reader as close as possible to the original text by providing:

1. The poem in Russian with the stress marks.
2. A side-by-side, unembellished version in English, matching the meaning as precisely as possible without sounding unnatural.
3. Commentary on difficult phrases and syntax, wordplay and neologisms, and clarification of cultural, historical and literary references.
4. Short essays exploring theme, persona and poetic technique.

Mayakovsky was a prolific writer, and it would take more time than I have left on the planet to translate every poem I wanted to. In this book, in order to give the reader "maximum access" to each work, I've limited the selection to just 24 of his best-known poems, representative of each stage of his career, "flashing and burning" points along the plumage of a "golden-born comet," the force of nature that was Mayakovsky.

A hurricane,
                    fire,
                         water
approach in a roar.
Who
     can control it?
You?
     Go ahead and try…

Из у́лицы в у́лицу

У́-
лица.
Ли́ца
У
до́гов
годо́в
ре́з-
че.
Че́
рез
желе́зных коне́й
с о́кон бегу́щих домо́в
пры́гнули пе́рвые ку́бы.
Ле́беди шей колоко́льных
гни́тесь в си́лках проводо́в!
В не́бе жира́фий рису́нок гото́в
вы́пестрить ржа́вые чу́бы.
Пёстер, как форе́ль,
сын
безузо́рной па́шни.
Фо́кусник
ре́льсы
тя́нет из па́сти трамва́я,
скрыт цифербла́тами ба́шни.
Мы завоёваны!
Ва́нны.
Ду́ши.
Лифт.
Лиф души́ расстегну́ли!
Те́ло жгут ру́ки.
Кричи́ не кричи́:
«я не хоте́ла!» —
ре́зок
жгут
му́ки.
Ве́тер колю́чий
трубе́
вырыва́ет
ды́мчатой ше́рсти клок.

From street to street

A
street.
Mastiff
faces
are
sharp-
er
than years.
O-
ver
iron horses
the first cubes leapt
from windows of running houses.
Swans of bell necks
curve yourselves in cable nooses!
In the sky a cartoon giraffe is ready
to show off motley rusty forelocks.
The son
of unploughed fields
is dappled like a trout.
A magician,
hidden by clock-tower faces,
is pulling rails
out of the streetcar's mouth.
We've been conquered!
Bathtubs.
Showers.
An elevator.
The soul's bodice is undone.
Hands burn your body.
Go ahead and scream:
"I didn't mean to!"
the tourniquet
of torment
is harsh.
The thorny wind
tears
a clump of smoky wool
from a chimney.

Лы́сый фона́рь
сладостра́стно снима́ет
с у́лицы
чёрный чуло́к.

1913

A bald streetlight
lavisciously pulls off
the street's
black stocking.

Из улицы в улицу/From street to street

M wrote his earliest poems while he was still an art student, and the painterly influence is clear. In school he had connected with a wild group of artists and poets—David Burliuk, Velimir Khlebnikov, Mikhail Larionov, Natalia Goncharova, Kazimir Malevich and Aleksey Kruchenykh, to name a few—who would become known as the Russian Futurists. The Futurists, deeply inspired by Picasso and Braque, took on the mission of upgrading Cubism by merging it with movement. Malevich achieved this on canvas in his painting *The Knife Grinder*, and M achieved it in poetic form in "From Street to Street."

True to Cubist principles, the images in "From street to street" are vivid and fragmented, depicted from multiple viewpoints, and appear in a disjointed, seemingly illogical sequence. Sentences—even words—are also fragmented, splitting across multiple lines. And the poem moves—one image displaces the next via the mechanism of a shared sound (бегущих домов/силках проводов/; фо-рель/рельсы; пашни/пасти трамвая/циферблатами башни; завоёваны/Ванны; шерсти клок/чёрный чулок). Aside from the literal images of transport (a street, horses, cables, rails, a streetcar, an elevator) and the frenetic objects (leaping cubes, the running houses, curving cables), the words themselves go back and forth and even up and down (У-лица/Лица У; догов/годов; рез-че/Че-рез; коней/окон; Души. Лифт/Лиф души, Тело жгут руки/резок жгут муки). [1]

с окон бегущих домов прыгнули первые кубы/the first cubes jumped from the windows of running houses

In his essay "How to Write Poetry," M mentions that this poem was inspired by the streetcar route from Sukharev tower to Sretensky Gates Square. Without this bit of information it would be difficult to make sense of this poem, but now we can imagine that the cubes are reflections from glass window panes that seem to jump as the streetcar moves by the buildings on Sretensky Blvd.

выпестрить ржавые чубы/to dapple rusty locks

One of M's signature moves is the creation of new verbal forms by tacking on nonstandard prefixes. A particular favorite is the prefix "вы" (here indicating the application of some kind of substance, as in "выкрасить/to apply paint," and "вымазать/to smear"), which he has appended to "пестрить/make gaudy."

Though the stress for "чубы/bangs" is normally on the 2nd syllable, I'm following

(1) For an in-depth study, see: Gregory Amelin, "Leksia VI," *Lekcii po filosofii literatury*. (Moscow, 2005), 113-147.

Lilya Brik's rendition of the poem, recorded in the late 50's by her 3rd husband, the historian Vasily Katanyan.

Лебеди шей колокольных гнитесь в силках проводов!/Swans of bell necks, curve yourselves in the nooses of cables!
Perhaps the shapes of a giraffe, swan necks and bells are discernable in the tangle of electric cables overhead. Both the phrase and romantic image of "swan necks" have been disassembled. The normal usage, "шеи лебедей," has been inverted, the necks belong to bells, and the instead of gracefully floating on a lake, the swans are hanging in the air, entangled in wires.

Фокусник рельсы тянет из пасти трамвая/A magician is pulling rails from the mouth of the streetcar
As if he's sitting in the back of the streetcar, watching the rails as they extend from Sukharev tower.

циферблатами башни/clock-towers faces
The 7-foot clock-faces of Sukharev tower were affixed in 1899. The weights attached to the gears weighed over 1800 pounds, and required weekly elevation from the base of the tower to the 4th floor ceiling for rewinding. There were also bells -- a giant one, which was struck on the hour, and smaller ones, which played a melody on the quarter hour. The tower, built by Peter I, was a major Moscow landmark until it was demolished in 1934, a sacrifice to Stalin's monolithic architectural vision for the capital.

Кричи не кричи/Go ahead and scream
Literally "scream don't scream," an example of a standard idiomatic form: "scream all you want, it won't make any difference."

А вы могли́ бы?

Я сра́зу сма́зал ка́рту бу́дня,
плесну́вши кра́ску из стака́на;
я показа́л на блю́де сту́дня
косы́е ску́лы океа́на.
На чешуе́ жестя́ной ры́бы
прочёл я зо́вы но́вых губ.
А вы
ноктю́рн сыгра́ть
могли́ бы
на фле́йте водосто́чных труб?

1913

And could you?

I promptly smeared the workday map,
splashing paint out of a glass;
I revealed the sharp cheek-bones of the ocean
on a platter of jellied meat.
I read the summons of new lips
on the scale of a tin fish.
And you—
could you
play a nocturne
on a drain-pipe flute?

А вы могли бы?/And could you?

Three weeks before his death in 1930, M gave his last public performance at a large technical institute in Moscow.(1) The audience, mostly students, was combative and at times even hostile. One of the more aggressive students kept standing up to insist that M's poetry made no sense. To prove his point, he read examples of M's early poetry, including "And could you," then yelled "Does all of this have any relationship to the revolution? Everything's written about yourself. It's all incomprehensible." M brushed aside the criticism with a comment that the poem "should be obvious to any proletariat. If a proletariat doesn't understand, then he's simply illiterate." And the message of "And could you" does seem obvious enough: the artist finds beauty and meaning amidst the mundanity of everyday life. But the heckler may have been pointing to something deeper: namely the rift between M's early poetic persona and the post-revolutionary proletarian audience of 1930.

When M wrote this poem in 1913 he and his friends were putting an idea known as "theater of life" into practice.(2) For the Cubo-Futurists, there was no division between life and art—life *was* art. To express this, they painted their faces with hieroglyphs, dogs and airplanes; they paraded along the fashionable streets of Moscow costumed in top hats, rags, garish ties and wooden spoons as boutonnières, shouting out poetry; Natalia Goncharova popped up at exhibitions bare-chested, her torso adorned only with paint. They conducted themselves in public as if performing on stage. "And could you" is a "theater of life" poem: the artist transforms the "map of workdays" into a painting, discovers oceanic cheekbones in a plate of jelly, reads a proclamation on a fish scale, and creates music from a drain pipe.

"And could you" is not only a demonstration of artistic philosophy, it's a confrontation. The aggressive adolescent/poet-hooligan is a dominant poetic persona in M's early canon, and though there are more extreme examples (e.g. in "Take that!" the poet threatens to spit in the audience's face), this is a gauntlet thrown to the feet of polite society. The Futurists, whose public debut was a manifesto entitled *A Slap in the Face of Public Taste*, made it their mission to upset bourgeois convention.

---

(1) M committed suicide on April 14th 1930. Three weeks before, on March 25, he delivered his last address to the Krasnaya Presnya Komsomol Club, at an evening dedicated to the exhibition *20 Years' Work*. Quotes are from V. I. Slavinsky, "Poslednia vystuplenia Vladimira Maiakovskovo," *V. Maiakovskii v vospominaniiakh sovremenikov*. (Moscow, 1963).

(2) For a thorough discussion, see: John E. Bowlt, "Natalia Goncharova and Futurist Theater" *Art Journal* Vol. 49, No. 1, (Spring, 1990): pp. 44-51. http://www.jstor.org/stable/777179 (accessed September 13, 2016).

Their performances were dangerous: the artists would loudly argue with the crowd; splash tea out into the theater seats; people would jump up on the stage; performers would jump into the audience; spectators had their faces insulted, slapped and painted. There was heckling, booing and pelting of bottles. Fights would break out, police would arrive, performances would be shut down in mid-sentence.

By 1930 the conditions that had made this poem relevant had vanished. M's avant-garde circle had been scattered to the winds—some emigrated; some died from war, disease and starvation; some were deported, arrested or shot; others suppressed their artistic urges and submitted to the constraints of Soviet society. The audience too was long gone—that set of bourgeois ladies and gentlemen amusing themselves in smart salons and cafes had been utterly destroyed. It's not surprising that "And could you" would be "incomprehensible" to a young student in 1930—it was a poem from another world.

будня/of the work day
A normal working day, as opposed to a holiday. It's unusual to see будень in the singular—normally it's in the plural (будни).

на блюде студня/on a plate of jellied meat
Studen, also known as *Kholodets*, is meat served in jellied stock—a traditional Russian dish.

На чешуе жестяной рыбы/On the scale of a tin fish
Considering the references to street signs from other poems ("Мой университет/My university," where the poet learned "the alphabet from street signs, turning over pages of iron and tin," and from "Вывескам/To street signs," where the reader is commanded to "read iron books"), we can infer that the tin fish here is a storefront sign.

Вы́вескам

Чита́йте желе́зные кни́ги!
Под фле́йту золо́ченой бу́квы
поле́зут копчёные си́ги
и золотоку́дрые брю́квы.

А е́сли весёлостью пёсьей
закру́жат созве́здия «Ма́гги» —
бюро́ похоро́нных проце́ссий
свои́ проведу́т саркофа́ги.

Когда́ же, хмур и плаче́вен,
зага́сит фона́рные зна́ки,
влюбля́йтесь под не́бом харче́вен
в фая́нсовых ча́йников ма́ки!

1913

To street signs

Read iron books!
Smoked whitefish and turnips with golden, curly locks
will climb
under a flute of a golden letter.

And if constellations of "Maggi" begin to whirl
with a dog-like joy—
the offices of funeral processions
will lead out their sarcophagi.

And when, sullen and tearful,
he puts out the lantern signs,
fall in love with Delft teapot poppies
under the sky of taverns!

Вывескам/To street signs

Though M claimed that he "knew nothing of meter,"[1] many of his early poems follow a standard rhythmic pattern, usually four foot iambs, or, like this one, three foot amphibrachs.[2] It's as if he were using training wheels before breaking out into the declamatory rhythms of his mature work.

Even rarer than the near-perfect amphibrachic meter is the cheery tone—there's no trace of the contempt, violence or grotesqueness that mark many other early poems. There are a few dark notes (sarcophagi from the funeral home, a sad and sullen someone who extinguishes the street lights), but the buoyant rhythm, the joyous opening and closing commands (Read iron books!", "Fall in love!"), the upward movement towards stars and sky, and the bright imagery make the poem "whirl with a doglike joy."

The biggest surprise is not the rhythm or the upbeat tone, but the poem's particular style of urbanism. Urban themes were nothing new in Russian poetry—street lights, streetcars, store windows, apartment buildings and city crowds had been familiar images since Nekrasov. What sets M apart is not just his intimacy with the streets of Moscow, but his utter embrace of them. In a lecture from 1912 entitled *Attainments of Futurism*, M declared that "the poetry of Futurism is the poetry of the modern city," that "we know nothing of forest, fields and flowers," but that "telephones, aeroplanes, express trains, elevators, rotary presses, sidewalks, factory smokestacks, masses of stone, soot and smoke – these are the elements of beauty in the new nature, urban nature." The "elements" in this poem are city street signs, and most surprisingly, one featuring the product name and logo for "Maggi" bouillon cubes. This is surely the first appearance of an international brand name in Russian poetry.

Под флейту золоченой буквы/Under a flute of a golden letter
"Под флейту" also means "accompanied by a flute."

---

(1) Vladimir Mayakovsky, "Kak delat' stikhi," (1926). Excerpts are from "How Are Verses Made?" in *Volodya: Selected Works*, edited by Rosy Carrick (Enitharmon Press, 2015), 224-237.

(2) In iambic meter, every other syllable is stressed, as in: "I do not like green eggs and ham./I do not like them, Sam-I-am." In amphibrachic meter, every middle syllable is stressed, as in: "And, speaking of birds, there's the Russian Palooski, /Whose headski is redski and belly is blueski." A foot is one rhythmic unit—for iamb, the unit is 2 syllables; for amphibrachs, the unit is 3 syllables.

The stress for золоченой is usually on the 3rd syllable (золочёной), but here is it on the 2nd.

созвездия «Магги»/constellations of Maggi
The logo for the Swiss food company Maggi features a red four-pointed star.

Когда же, хмур и плачевен, загасит фонарные знаки/And when, sullen and tearful, he puts out the lantern signs
This couplet presents a puzzle: who is the unnamed masculine subject? Perhaps a lamp lighter (фонарщик)? Or perhaps that same force which puts out the stars? And what, exactly, are "lantern signs"? The short form adjective "плачевен" is also peculiar, since it's never used to describe a person, but only an event, as in "a deplorable development, a lamentable result."

Ади́ще го́рода

Ади́ще го́рода о́кна разби́ли
на кро́хотные, сосу́щие све́тами адки́.
Ры́жие дья́волы, вздыма́лись автомоби́ли,
над са́мым у́хом взрыва́я гудки́.

А там, под вы́веской, где се́льди из Ке́рчи —
сби́тый старика́шка ша́рил очки́
и запла́кал, когда́ в вечере́ющем сме́рче
трамва́й с разбе́га взметну́л зрачки́.

В ды́рах небоскрёбов, где горе́ла руда́
и желе́зо поездо́в громозди́ло лаз —
кри́кнул аэропла́н и упа́л туда́,
где у ра́неного со́лнца вытека́л глаз.

И тогда́ уже́ — ско́мкав фонаре́й одея́ла —
ночь излюби́лась, поха́бна и пьяна́,
а за со́лнцами у́лиц где-то ковыля́ла
никому́ не ну́жная, дря́блая луна́.

1913

A monstrous hell of a city

Windows smashed the monstrous hell of the city
into tiny hells sucking with light.
Red devils, automobiles heave,
blasting horns right into your ear.

And there, under the street sign for Kerch herring,
a old man, knocked down, groped for glasses—
and started crying when the tram
going full speed in the evening whirlwind
swept up its pupils.

In the gaps of skyscrapers, where ore was blazing
and the iron of trains piled up at a tunnel
an aeroplane screamed and fell
where the injured sun's eye was dripping out.

And only then—wadding up the blanket of street lamps—
night loved itself out, smutty and drunk,
and somewhere behind the street suns
hobbled a flaccid moon, wanted by no one.

Адище города/A monstrous hell of a city

The critic Korney Chukovsky might have had this poem in mind when he said that for Mayakovsky "the city is not a delight, not a drunken joy, but a crucifixion, Golgotha, a crown of thorns, and every city vision is like a nail driven into his heart."(1)

"A Monstrous Hell" is very different from "To Street Signs" in meter, tone and imagery. Here the rhythm is more "Mayakovskian": roughly amphibrachic, with 4 stresses per line; but unpredictable, choppy, abrupt. As opposed to the happy sounds of the previous poem (o's and a's; b's v's and f's), here we have buzzing and scraping consonant clusters (щ/shch з/z ч/ch/зб кр/kr зд/zd взр/vzr чк/chk), and a repeated, squealing "и". The objects are fractured, moving, dangerous: sucking window shards, heaving automobiles blasting their horns, trams with sweeping pupils, screaming aeroplanes. It fills M's prescription for writing modern poetry:

> "We . . . are familiar with tunnels of streets and their movement, noise, thunder, flashing, eternal gyrations. . . (T)he rhythm of life has changed. Everything has become lightning-like, transient, like a reel of film. The smooth, peaceful, unhurried rhythms of the old poetry don't correspond to the psyche of the modern citizen. Feverish activity —that's . . . the tempo of modernity. In the city there are no smooth, even, circular lines: corners, fractures, zigzags—that's what characterizes the image of the city. Poetry must comply with the new elements of the modern city's psyche."(2)

окна разбили на крохотные, сосущие светами адки́.
It seems the sun is setting and the light reflecting from the windows is fragmenting into little shards.

сбитый/hit
The standard verbal adjective for "hit by a vehicle"

В дырах небоскрёбов/in the gaps of skyscrapers
This city hellscape is not recognizable as Moscow or Petersburg—the only skyscrapers of the day were in New York and Chicago.

---

(1) Korney Chukovsky. "Futuristy," *Litsa i maski* (Shipovnik, 1914), as cited by Dmitry Bykov. *Trinadcatii apostol. Mayakovskii: Tragediya-buff v shesti dejstviyah.* (Young Guard, 2016) 184-195.

(2) From M's speech "The Attainments of Futurism." *Mayakovskiy Vladimir Vladimirovich: Polnoe sobranie sochineniy.* Maksim Moshkow and the Federal Agency of Print and Mass Communication. http://az.lib.ru/m/majakowskij_w_w/text_0120.shtml (accessed January 15, 2017).

железо поездов громоздило лаз/the iron of trains piled up at a tunnel

An ambiguous phrase, since in normal use "громоздить" is transitive ("the iron of trains piled up the tunnel"). But here it seems to be intransitive ("piling itself up"). The image is of trains crowding around the mouth of narrow tunnel, unable to squeeze in all at once. "Лаз" can be a tunnel either for animals or for mining, but in this case, the earlier reference to "blazing ore" supports the mining interpretation.

ночь излюбилась/the night loved itself out

A pretty rude and unappetizing phrase, as if night were a prostitute worn out by a long evening of work. The poem too has "loved itself out" in this last stanza: a "flaccid" moon hobbles away, and the scraping and squealing has been replaced by sounds of exhaustion: l's, m's, n's and ah's.

а за солнцами улиц/behind the suns of the street

The image of streets with their man-made suns is very modernistic, and a good illustration of M's point that "the city is replacing nature and its elements," and that "the civilized word is turning into one gigantic city." The city is surging with demonic power—the wounded sun and flaccid moon are defeated, weak and useless.

Кое-что про Петербург

Слеза́ют слёзы с кры́ши в тру́бы,
к руке́ реки́ чертя́ поло́ски;
а в не́ба сви́сшиеся гу́бы
воткну́ли ка́менные со́ски.

И не́бу — сти́хши — я́сно ста́ло:
туда́, где мо́ря бле́щет блю́до,
сыро́й пого́нщик гнал уста́ло
Невы́ двуго́рбого верблю́да.

1913

Еще Петербург

В уша́х обры́вки тёплого ба́ла,
а с се́вера — снега́ седе́й —
тума́н, с кровожа́дным лицо́м канниба́ла,
жева́л невку́сных люде́й.

Часы́ нависа́ли, как гру́бая брань,
за пя́тым нави́с шесто́й.
А с не́ба смотре́ла кака́я-то дрянь
вели́чественно, как Лев Толсто́й.

1914

Something about Petersburg

Tears climb down the roof into drain pipes,
drawing furrows to the arm of the river;
and stone pacifiers were shoved
into lips hanging down from the sky.

And, quieting down, the sky could clearly see:
there, where the dish of the sea sparkles;
a sodden driver was wearily urging on
the two-humped camel of the Neva.

Still Petersburg

In the ears are fragments of a warm dance,
and from the north—greyer than snow—
the fog, with a cannibal's blood-thirsty face,
chewed on bad-tasting people.

The hours loomed like crude profanity,
the sixth hung behind the fifth.
And from the sky some piece of trash looked on
majestically, like Leo Tolstoy.

Кое-что про Петербург/Something about Petersburg

Though M spent most of his life in Moscow, Petersburg was the site of his earliest Futurist adventures: readings at the Stray Dog Cafe; a lecture at the Troitsky Theater, where offended audience members climbed on stage and tried to drag him off; sold-out performances of *Vladimir Mayakovsky, a Tragedy* in Luna Park. Petersburg is where M fell in love with Lilya Brik, where he published "A cloud in trousers," where he wrote "Backbone-flute," "Man," and "War and the universe." He lived in Petersburg from 1915-1918, both with the Briks and also in his own apartment on Nadezhdinskaya Street, which was renamed in 1936—it's now known as Mayakovsky Street.

In these two poems, M tackles a couple of classic Petersburg themes: the terrible weather and the city's illusionary, nightmarish quality. Since Pushkin's "The Bronze Horseman," Russian writers have been tormenting their Petersburg characters not only with freezing rain, fog, and floods, but with supernatural sword-wielding statues, noses in uniform and menacing doppelgangers. Here nature is surreal, grotesque and threatening: the sky is crying, its hanging lips suck on rooftop pacifiers, the two-humped river has arms, a blood-thirsty fog descends from the north to chew on people.

свисшиеся/having hung themselves down

"Свисать/свиснуть" doesn't exist in the reflexive, and though there is the participle "свисший," it's rarely used.

Еще Петербург/Still Petersburg

The original title of this poem was "Утро Петербурга/A Petersburg morning." This helps us put things in context: the poet has been out all night and is still roaming the streets at 6 am.

Часы нависали . . . за пятым навис шестой/the sixth hung behind the fifth
"Часы" could be clock, but the meaning here is probably hours. From the adjective endings of fifth and sixth, it's clear that the unmentioned noun is "час/hour." It seems that the clock has just struck six (the expression in Russian is "пробил шесть"), and the sound is lingering in the air.

какая-то дрянь/some piece of trash
An early and typical example of blasphemy, not only against God, but also against the gods of Russian literature. The Futurists came out swinging against the literary establishment, demanding that "Pushkin, Dostoevsky, Tolstoy, etc., etc." be thrown off the "Ship of Modernity;" mocking Balmont for his "perfumed lechery" and Bryusov for his posturing as a mystic warrior, his cardboard armor shining with the "dawn of unknown beauties;" advising the public to "wash the hands which have touched the filthy slime of the books written by countless Leonid Andreyevs . . . Maxim Gorkys, Krupins, Bloks, Sologubs, Remizovs, Averchenkos, Chornys, Kuzmins, Bunins . . . "(1)

(1) Vladimir Mayakovsky et al, *Poshch'ochna obshchestvennomu vkusu.* (1912). Full text is available on *Mayakovskiy Vladimir Vladimirovich: Polnoe sobranie sochineniy.* Maksim Moshkow and the Federal Agency of Print and Mass Communication. http://az.lib.ru/m/majakowskij_w_w/text_0150.shtml (accessed January 20, 2017).

Ко́фта фа́та

Я сошью́ себе́ чёрные штаны́
из ба́рхата го́лоса моего́.
Жёлтую ко́фту из трёх арши́н зака́та.
По Не́вскому ми́ра, по лощёным полоса́м его́,
профлани́рую ша́гом Дон-Жуа́на и фа́та.

Пусть земля́ кричи́т, в поко́е оба́бившись:
«Ты зелёные вёсны идёшь наси́ловать!»
Я бро́шу со́лнцу, на́гло оскла́бившись:
«На гла́ди асфа́льта мне хорошо́ грасси́ровать!»

Не потому́ ли, что не́бо голубо́,
а земля́ мне любо́вница в э́той пра́здничной чи́стке,
я дарю́ вам стихи́, весёлые, как би-ба-бо,
и о́стрые и ну́жные, как зубочи́стки!

Же́нщины, лю́бящие моё мя́со, и э́та
де́вушка, смотря́щая на меня́, как на бра́та,
закида́йте улы́бками меня́, поэ́та, —
я цвета́ми нашью́ их мне на ко́фту фа́та!

1914

The fop's smock

I'll sew myself a pair of black trousers
from the velvet of my voice.
A yellow smock from three yards of sunset.
I'll saunter along the Nevsky Prospect of the world, along its polished strips,
with the step of Don Juan and a fop.

Let the earth, gone past her prime, yell out:
"You're going off to rape the green springs!"
I throw a taunt at the sun, brazenly grinning,
"It good to roll my r's along the smooth surface of the asphalt!"

Isn't it because the sky is blue
and the earth is my lover in this holiday cleaning
that I give you verses? Amusing, like bi-ba-bo,
and sharp and useful like toothpicks!

Women, who love my meat, and this
girl, who looks at me like I'm her brother,
shower your smiles on me, the poet,
I'll sew them onto my smock like flowers.

Кофта фата/The fop's smock

M's standard performance attire before 1915 included a bright, loose, yellow shirt resembling an artist's smock, accessorized with a garish homemade tie and a silk top hat. The Futurists made a point to dress outrageously, but for M there was an additional motive:

> "Few knew that in those years M was completely impoverished. He happily made the best of this, enduring his circumstances with the proud bearing of a millionaire and a 'fop.' In his room the only furniture, so to speak, was a nail, from which hung his yellow smock and where his top hat also took shelter. There wasn't even a table. But he didn't feel the necessity of a table—he barely had enough for a daily meal."(1)

The newspapers referred to M as the "hooligan in a yellow blouse," and this is the persona he assumes in this poem. His lyrical "I" is fully formed, and going forward, he nearly always casts himself in the leading role of hero/martyr/clown. As Pasternak put it, "the poet was not the author but the subject of the lyric, who addressed the world in the first person singular."

The "Mayakovskian" rhythm is fully developed here—a completely unpredictable mix of anapests, dactyls, trochees and iambs, with a random number of stresses per line. This is the rhythm of oration, of emphatic conversation, of performance.

Невский/Nevsky

Nevsky Prospect is the main thoroughfare in St. Petersburgh, but in this poem, it's more than that – it's the *greatest* boulevard in the *greatest* city in the world. There's a sense of exaltation: a young male inscribing himself into the cosmos.

в покое обабившись/having gone past her prime in inactivity

Who, left in peace, lost her girlish figure (imagine Natasha in *War and Peace*, after marrying Pierre and having 4 childen.)

---

(1) Korney Chukovsky, "Maiakovskii" *V. Maiakovskii v vospominaniiakh sovremenikov*. (Moscow, 1963).

Ты зелёные вёсны идёшь насиловать/You're going off to rape green springs

The earth, who in the next stanza we discover is his lover, is angry because she expects the poet to go molest the young nymphs of spring? Her daughters, maybe? Like most of M's early poems, this one contains something crude and jarring. Whether, as in this example, it's sexual assault, or grotesque insults ("you peer out like an oyster from ... thick white makeup," "your flaccid fat will flow ... out onto the street", or "I'll ... spit in your faces" from "Take that"), or misanthropy ("I like watching children die" from "A few words about myself"), or blasphemy (God runs around in the sky panting for breath in "But be that as is may") or just plain ugliness (poems are populated with slime, cigarette butts, drool, syphilis, prostitutes running from burning houses, swollen flesh, veiny hands, hundred-headed louses with bristling little legs; things are wadded up, oozing, flabby, stupid, decrepit, disgusting, shriveled), the intent is perhaps not only to shock and to challenge, but to assert the poet's status as a Nietzschean hero above the laws of conventional society.

На глади асфальта/On the smooth surface of the asphalt

"Гладь/smoothness" is generally associated with water and nature, not asphalt.

Грассировать/To roll one's r's

To roll one's r's in the French manner, characteristic of the upper class.

Би-ба-бо/bi-ba-bo

Hand puppets. This noun is indeclinable, and here it's in the plural.

Женщины, любящие моё мясо/women, who love my meat

More crudeness, as "мясо/meat" is much stronger than "плоть/flesh." "Мясо" can refer to human bodies, as in "пушечное мясо/cannon fodder," but M is using it, idiosyncratically, in a sexual context.

Я брошу солнцу/I taunt the sun

A shortened form of "бросить слово," meaning "to speak nonchalantly." It's not necessarily rude, but a curt phrase without much care.

Вот так я сде́лался соба́кой

Ну, это соверше́нно невыноси́мо!
Весь как есть иску́сан зло́бой.
Злюсь не так, как могли́ бы вы:
как соба́ка лицо́ луны́ гололо́бой —
взял бы
и всё обвы́л.

Не́рвы, должно́ быть...
Вы́йду,
погуля́ю.
И на у́лице не успоко́ился ни на ком я.
Кака́я-то прокрича́ла про до́брый ве́чер.
На́до отве́тить:
она́ — знако́мая.
Хочу́.
Чу́вствую —
не могу́ по-челове́чьи.

Что это за безобра́зие?
Сплю я, что ли?
Ощу́пал себя́:
тако́й же, как был,
лицо́ тако́е же, к како́му привы́к.
Тро́нул губу́,
а у меня́ из-под губы́ —
клык.

Скоре́е закры́л лицо́, как бу́дто сморка́юсь.
Бро́сился к до́му, шаги́ удво́ив.
Бе́режно огиба́ю полице́йский пост,
вдруг оглуши́тельное:
«Городово́й!
Хвост!»

Провёл руко́й и - остолбене́л!
Э́того-то,
вся́ких клыко́в почи́ще,
я не заме́тил в бе́шеном ска́че:
у меня́ из-под пиджака́

And that's how I became a dog

Well, this is really unbearable!
All of me chewed up by spite
I don't get enraged the way you would:
I'd up and
howl it all to bits—
like a hound at the bare-browed face of the moon.

Nerves, probably . . .
I'll go out,
have a little walk.
But no one on the street gave me any relief.
Some woman shouted about good evening.
I have to respond:
She's someone I know.
I want to.
But I feel—
I just can't speak human.

What kind of disgrace is this!?
Am I dreaming?
I patted myself:
same as before,
the same face that I'm used to.
I touched my lip,
and underneath my lip—
was a fang.

I quickly covered my face, like I was blowing my nose.
I rushed home, doubling my pace.
I carefully cut around the policeman's beat,
and suddenly there's a deafening:
"Officer!
A tail!"

I passed my hand over—and froze!
In my mad gallop I didn't notice
this thing,
more serious than any fang,
from under my jacket

развéерился хвости́ще
и вьётся сзáди,
большóй, собáчий.

Что тепéрь?
Оди́н заорáл, толпý растя́.
Вторóму прибáвился трéтий, четвёртый.
Смя́ли старушóнку.
Онá, крестя́сь, что-то кричáла про чёрта.

И когдá, ощети́нив в лицó уси́ща-вéники,
толпá навали́лась,
огрóмная,
злáя,
я стал на четверéньки
и залáял:
Гав! гав! гав!

1914

a tail was fanning out
and curling up from behind,
big, doggish.

Now what?
Someone began to yell, raising a crowd.
A second was joined by a third, a forth.
They crushed an old woman.
Crossing herself, she yelled out something about the devil.

And when, bristling up their mustache-brooms in my face,
the crowd fell on me,
huge,
malicious,
I stood on all fours
and started barking:
Arf! Arf! Arf!

Вот так я сделался собакой/And that's how I became a dog

M's poetry is packed with all kinds of animals—elephants, giraffes, gorillas, baby whales, camels, parrots—but it seems he identified most strongly with dogs. Lilya Brik nicknamed him "Shchen," short for puppy ("щенок"), and his letters to her often included sketches of himself as a little floppy-eared dog—on the prow of a boat, looking out to sea, on a mountain with a shish kebab, perched in a palm tree looking through binoculars. In this poem, however, the dog is not so cute.

This is very different poem than "The Fop's Smock" in both persona and tone. The ultra-confident hero of "Fop" is now anxious, self-conscious, and vulnerable. The celebratory, emphatic rhythm of "Fop" is also gone—now we have isolated words and phrases occupying single lines, in what's called "ladder," "column" or "stolbik" format. This layout encourages the poem to be read with the pauses, stresses and intonations of conversation. This is the rhythm of internal dialog—a man talking to himself in clipped phrases, alternating between words of self-assurance and cries of alarm.

Весь как есть/Everything as is
An idiom meaning "all of me."

обвыл/howl
"Выть" is usually associated not with dogs, but with wolves. M has added the non-standard prefix "об," which also happens to be the prefix for "оборотень/werewolf." The howling is inspired by the "bare-faced" moon, which may also be the impetus for this transformation of man into beast.

И на улице не успокоился ни на ком я/No one on the street provided any relief
An unusual phrase, literally "On the street I couldn't find anyone to calm down on." The set phrase, which you'd only hear from a fortune-teller laying out her cards, is "Что есть, что будет и... на ком сердце успокоится?" "What is, what will be, who will ease your heart?"

Хвост!/A Tail!
As in English, a "tail" can refer to an undercover officer who follows a suspect.

почище/even more
A colloquial expression meaning "even greater."

развеерился/fanned itself out
M has created a reflexive verb from the noun "веер" (fan).

толпа навалилась/the crowd fell on me
This is not the only time M assumes the form of a suffering animal—in "To Russia," he's an ostrich in Siberia with "feathers of rhythm and rhyme"; in "About that," he's a polar bear floating down the Neva on a chunk of ice; in "Backbone Flute," he's a fatally wounded bull, gazing at his beloved through a dying eye. This is a favorite device for presenting a favorite theme: the poet/martyr is misunderstood, unappreciated and ultimately persecuted by the philistine crowd.

Фле́йта-позвоно́чник

Проло́г

За всех вас,
кото́рые нра́вились и́ли нра́вятся,
храни́мых ико́нами у души́ в пеще́ре,
как ча́шу вина́ в засто́льной здра́вице,
подъе́млю стиха́ми напо́лненный че́реп.

Всё ча́ще ду́маю –
не поста́вить ли лу́чше
то́чку пу́ли в своём конце́.
Сего́дня я
на вся́кий слу́чай
даю́ проща́льный конце́рт.

Па́мять!
Собери́ у мо́зга в за́ле
люби́мых неисчерпа́емые о́череди.
Смех из глаз в глаза́ лей.
Былы́ми сва́дьбами ночь ряди́.
Из те́ла в те́ло весе́лье ле́йте.
Пусть не забу́дется ночь нике́м.
Я сего́дня бу́ду игра́ть на фле́йте.
На со́бственном позвоно́чнике.

1

Ве́рсты у́лиц взма́хами шаго́в мну.
Куда́ уйду́ я, э́тот ад тая́!
Како́му небе́сному Го́фману
вы́думалась ты, прокля́тая?!

Бу́ре весе́лья у́лицы у́зки.
Пра́здник наря́дных черпа́л и че́рпал.
Ду́маю.
Мы́сли, кро́ви сгу́стки,
больны́е и запёкшиеся, ле́зут из че́репа.

Backbone-flute

Prologue

To all of you,
who I love or have loved,
watched over by icons in the cave of my soul,
I raise my skull, filled with poetry,
like a chalice of wine before the table.

More and more often I think—
wouldn't it be better
to punctuate my end with a bullet.
Just in case,
today I
am giving my farewell concert.

Memory!
Gather the inexhaustible rows of beloveds
into the grand hall of my brain.
Pour laughter from eyes to eyes.
Deck the night with weddings of bygone days.
Pour gaiety from body to body.
Let no one forget this night.
Today I will play the flute—
my own backbone.

1

Trampling miles of streets in swinging strides.
Where can I go, harboring this hell?
What kind of celestial Hoffmann
conjured up you, cursed woman?!

The streets are too narrow for a storm of merriment.
The holiday keeps ladling out smartly dressed people.
I'm thinking.
Thoughts like blood clots,
painful and clotted, crawl out of my skull.

Мне,
чудотво́рцу всего́, что пра́здднично,
самому́ на пра́здник вы́йти не с кем.
Возьму́ сейча́с и гро́хнусь на́взничь
и го́лову вы́мозжу ка́менным Не́вским!
Вот я богоху́лил.
Ора́л, что бо́га нет,
а бог таку́ю из пе́кловых глуби́н,
что пе́ред ней гора́ заволну́ется и дро́гнет,
вы́вел и веле́л:
люби́!

Бог дово́лен.
Под не́бом в кру́че
изму́ченный челове́к одича́л и вы́мер.
Бог потира́ет ладо́ни ру́чек.
Ду́мает бог:
погоди́, Влади́мир!
Э́то ему́, ему́ же,
чтоб не догада́лся, кто́ ты,
вы́думалось дать тебе́ настоя́щего му́жа
и на роя́ль положи́ть челове́чьи но́ты.
Е́сли вдруг подкра́сться к две́ри спа́ленной,
перекрести́ть над ва́ми стёганье одея́лово,
зна́ю —
запа́хнет ше́рстью па́ленной,
и се́рой издыми́тся мя́со дья́вола.

А я вме́сто э́того до утра́ ра́ннего
в у́жасе, что тебя́ люби́ть увели́,
мета́лся
и кри́ки в стро́чки выгра́нивал,
уже́ наполови́ну сумасше́дший ювели́р.
В ка́рты б игра́ть!
В вино́
вы́полоскать го́рло се́рдцу изо́ханному.
Не на́до тебя́!
Не хочу́!
Все равно́
я зна́ю,
я ско́ро сдо́хну.

I,
the creator of everything celebratory,
have no one to go celebrate with.
Maybe I'll just crash backwards
and debrain my head on the bricks of Nevsky.
I'm guilty of blasphemy.
I yelled there is no god,
And god brought forth from the scorching depths
such a creature
that a mountain would quiver before her in excitement,
and commanded: Love her!

God is pleased.
Under the sky on a steep slope
an exhausted man became savage and went extinct.
God rubs his little hands together.
God thinks:
Just wait, Vladimir!
It was him—he's the one
who came up with the idea of giving you a real husband
and setting a human score on the piano,
so that I wouldn't guess who you really were.
If someone snuck up to your bedroom door
and made the sign of the cross over you
I know
the stitching of your quilt would give off a smell of scorched fur,
and devil's meat would smolder and smoke like sulfur.

But instead I was delirious
and ran around until early morning, horrified
that someone else had taken you away to love,
and I cut my screams into verses like facets,
a jeweler, already half mad.
If I could escape into a card game!
If I could rinse the throat of my groaned-out heart
in wine!
I don't need you!
I don't want you!
I know
I'll croak soon enough
anyway.

Е́сли пра́вда, что есть ты,
бо́же,
бо́же мой,
е́сли звёзд ковёр тобо́ю вы́ткан,
е́сли э́той бо́ли,
ежедне́вно мно́жимой,
тобо́й ниспо́слана, го́споди, пы́тка,
суде́йскую цепь наде́нь.
Жди моего́ визи́та.
Я аккура́тный,
не заме́длю ни на день.
Слу́шай,
Всевы́шний инквизи́тор!

Рот зажму́.
Крик ни оди́н им
не вы́пущу из иску́санных губ я.
Привяжи́ меня́ к коме́там, как к хвоста́м лошади́ным,
и вы́мчи,
рвя о звёздные зу́бья.
Или вот что:
когда́ душа́ моя́ вы́селится,
вы́йдет на суд твой,
вы́хмурясь ту́пенько,
ты,
Мле́чный Путь переки́нув ви́селицей,
возьми́ и вздёрни меня́, престу́пника.
Де́лай, что хо́чешь.
Хо́чешь, четверту́й.
Я сам тебе́, пра́ведный, ру́ки вы́мою.
То́лько —
слы́шишь! —
убери́ прокля́тую ту,
кото́рую сде́лал мое́й люби́мою!

Вёрсты у́лиц взма́хами шаго́в мну.
Куда́ я де́нусь, это́т ад тая́!
Како́му небе́сному Го́фману
вы́думалась ты, прокля́тая?!

If it's true that you exist
god,
my god,
if the tapestry of stars was woven by you,
if this agony,
with its daily intensifying pain,
was sent down by you, lord,
then don your judge's chain.
Wait for my visit.
I'm punctual,
I won't delay even for a day
Listen,
Lord inquisitor!

I'll shut my mouth.
I won't let a single cry leave
my bitten lips.
Tie me to comets, like horse tails,
and send them racing away,
tearing on star teeth.
Or how about this:
when my soul vacates the premises,
and appears, sullen and frowning,
to receive your judgment,
you
throw a hangman's rope over the Milky Way,
take me and string me up, a criminal.
Do whatever you want.
Quarter me, if you want
I'll wash your hands myself, righteous one.
Only—
do you hear?—
Take away this cursed woman
that you made me love.

Trampling miles of streets in swinging strides.
Where can I go, harboring this hell?
What kind of celestial Hoffmann
conjured up you, cursed woman?!

2

И не́бо,
в дыма́х забы́вшее, что голубо́,
и ту́чи, обо́дранные бе́женцы то́чно,
вы́зарю в мою́ после́днюю любо́вь,
я́ркую, как румя́нец у чахо́точного.

Ра́достью покро́ю рёв
ско́па
забы́вших о до́ме и ую́те.
Лю́ди,
слу́шайте!
Вы́лезьте из око́пов.
По́сле довою́ете.

Да́же е́сли,
от кро́ви кача́ющийся, как Ба́хус,
пья́ный бой идёт —
слова́ любви́ и тогда́ не ве́тхи.
Ми́лые не́мцы!
Я зна́ю,
на губа́х у вас
гётевская Гре́тхен.
Францу́з,
улыба́ясь, на штыке́ мрёт,
с улы́бкой разбива́ется подстре́ленный авиа́тор,
е́сли вспо́мнят
в поцелу́е рот
твой, Травиа́та.

Но мне не до ро́зовой мя́коти,
кото́рую столе́тия вы́жуют.
Сего́дня к но́вым нога́м ля́гте!
Тебя́ пою́,
накра́шенную,
ры́жую.

Мо́жет быть, от дней э́тих,
жу́тких, как штыко́в острия́,
когда́ столе́тия вы́белят бо́роду,

2

I'll light the sky,
that's forgotten, in all the smoke, that it's blue,
and the clouds, ragged refugees,
in my last love,
blazing like the burning cheeks of a consumptive.

I'll cover the cry
of the crowd—those
who have forgotten home and comfort—with joy.
People,
Listen!
Climb out of the trenches.
You'll finish fighting later.

Even if,
staggering from blood, like Bacchus,
the drunken battle continues—
words of love don't wear out.
My dear Germans!
I know
Goethe's Gretchen
is on your lips.
A Frenchman
dies on a bayonet, smiling,
a wounded aviator crashes with a smile
if they remember
kissing your mouth,
Traviata.

But I don't want any rosy pulp
that'll be chewed on for a hundred years.
Lay down today at new feet!
I sing you,
my rouged
redhead.

Maybe, from these days,
as terrifying as bayonet points,
when the centuries whiten the beard,

оста́немся то́лько
ты
и я,
броса́ющийся за тобо́й от го́рода к го́роду.

Бу́дешь за́ море о́тдана,
спря́чешься у но́чи в норе́ —
я в тебя́ вцелу́ю сквозь тума́ны Ло́ндона
о́гненные гу́бы фонаре́й.

В зно́е пусты́ни вы́тянешь карава́ны,
где львы начеку́, —
тебе́
под пы́лью, ве́тром рва́ной,
положу́ Саха́рой горя́щую щеку́.

Улы́бку в гу́бы вло́жишь,
смо́тришь —
тореадо́р хоро́ш как!
И вдруг я
ре́вность метну́ в ло́жи
мру́щим гла́зом быка́.

Вы́несешь на́ мост шаг рассе́янный –
ду́мать,
хорошо́ внизу́ бы.
Э́то я
под мосто́м разли́лся Се́ной,
зову́,
ска́лю гнилы́е зу́бы.

С други́м зажгёшь в огне́ рысако́в
Стре́лку и́ли Соко́льники.
Э́то я, взобра́вшись туда́ высоко́,
луно́й томлю́, жду́щий и го́ленький.

Си́льный,
пона́доблюсь им я —
веля́т:
себя́ на войне́ убе́й!
После́дним бу́дет

there will only remain
you
and me,
dashing after you from city to city.

You'll be given in marriage beyond the sea,
you'll hide in the burrows of the night—
through the fog of London I'll kiss
the burning lips of street lights into you.

In the heat of the desert you'll stretch out caravans,
where lions stand guard—
under dust, ripped by the wind,
I will press my cheek, the burning Sahara,
to you.

You insert a smile into your lips
you look—
the toreador is so handsome!
And suddenly I'll
throw my jealously into the box seats
through the bull's dying eye.

You take a distracted step onto a bridge
and think
wouldn't it be nice to fall off.
I'm
the Seine, spread out under the bridge
I'm calling,
baring my rotten teeth.

You'll set fire to Strelka or Sokolniki with another man
in the flame of carriage horses.
I'm the moon, climbing up high,
eager and naked, making you languish.

I'm strong,
they'll need me—
they command:
go kill yourself in the war!
Your name

твоё и́мя,
запёкшееся на вы́дранной ядро́м губе́.

Коро́ной ко́нчу?
Свято́й Еле́ной?
Бу́ре жи́зни оседла́в валы́,
я — ра́вный кандида́т
и на царя́ вселе́нной
и на
кандалы́.

Быть царём назна́чено мне –
твоё ли́чико
на со́лнечном зо́лоте мои́х моне́т
велю́ наро́ду:
вы́чекань!
А там,
где ту́ндрой мир вы́линял,
где с се́верным ве́тром ведёт река́ торги́, —
на цепь нацара́паю и́мя Ли́лино
и цепь исцелу́ю во мра́ке ка́торги.

Слу́шайте ж, забы́вшие, что не́бо голубо́,
вы́щетинившиеся,
зве́ри то́чно!
Э́то, мо́жет быть,
после́дняя в ми́ре любо́вь
вы́зарилась румя́нцем чахо́точного.

3

Забу́ду год, день, число́.
Запру́сь одино́кий с листо́м бума́ги я.
Твори́сь, просветлённых страда́нием слов
нечелове́чья ма́гия!

Сего́дня, то́лько вошёл к вам,
почу́вствовал —
в до́ме нела́дно.
Ты что-то таи́ла в ше́лковом пла́тье,
и ши́рился в во́здухе за́пах ла́дана.

will be the last thing,
clotting with blood on my cannon torn lips.

Will I with a crown?
Or on St. Helena?
Having saddled the storm waves of life,
I'm an equal candidate
for king of the universe
and
for shackles.

If I am appointed king—
I will command the people
to mint
your face
on my coins' sunny gold.
And there,
where the world shed its skin to become the tundra
where the river haggles with the north wind,
I'll scratch the name Lilya on my chain
and kiss and kiss my chain in the darkness of a prison camp.

Listen, you who have forgotten that the sky is blue,
who have bristled up
just like beasts!
This may be
the last love in the world
and it shines like the burning cheeks of a consumptive.

3

I'll forget the year, the day, the date.
I'll lock myself up alone with a sheet of paper,
Arise, non-human magic of words
illuminated by suffering!

Today, as soon as I came to see you,
I felt
something in the house was wrong.
You were hiding something in your silk dress,
and funeral incense spread through the air.

Ра́да?
Холо́дное
«о́чень».
Смяте́ньем разби́та ра́зума огра́да.
Я отча́янье громозжу́, горя́щ и лихора́дочен.

Послу́шай,
всё равно́
не спря́чешь тру́па.
Стра́шное сло́во на го́лову лавь!
Всё равно́
твой ка́ждый му́скул
как в ру́пор
труби́т:
умерла́, умерла́, умерла́!
Нет,
отве́ть.
Не лги!
(Как я тако́й уйду́ наза́д?)
Я́мами двух моги́л
вы́рылись в лице́ твое́м глаза́.

Моги́лы глу́бятся.
Не́ту дна там.
Ка́жется,
ру́хну с помо́ста дней.
Я ду́шу над про́пастью натяну́л кана́том,
жонгли́руя слова́ми, закача́лся над ней.

Зна́ю,
любо́вь его́ износи́ла уже́.
Ску́ку уга́дываю по сто́льким при́знакам.
Вы́молоди себя́ в мое́й душе́.
Пра́зднику те́ла се́рдце вы́знакомь.

Зна́ю,
ка́ждый за же́нщину пла́тит.
Ничего́,
е́сли пока́
тебя́ вме́сто ши́ка пари́жских пла́тьев
оде́ну в дым табака́.

Happy to see me?
A cold
"very."
The wall of reason is demolished by panic.
Burning and feverish, I heap up despair.

Listen,
no matter what,
you can't hide a dead body.
Pour the awful words on my head like lava!
No matter what,
your every muscle
as if through a megaphone
proclaims:
It's dead! It's dead! It's dead!
No,
answer.
Don't lie!
(How can I leave like this?)
Your eyes have dug themselves
into your face like two open graves.

The graves deepen.
They have no bottom.
It seems
I'll crash down from the scaffolding of days.
I stretched my soul over the abyss like a tightrope,
I swayed on it, juggling words.

I know,
you've already worn out his love.
I detect the boredom from so many signs.
Rejuvenate yourself in my soul.
Acquaint your heart with the body's jubilation.

I know
everyone must pay for a woman.
It doesn't matter,
if for now,
instead of chic Parisian dresses,
I'll dress you in tobacco smoke.

Любо́вь мою́,
как апо́стол во вре́мя о́но,
по ты́сяче ты́сяч разнесу́ доро́г.
Тебе́ в века́х угото́вана коро́на,
а в коро́не слова́ мои́ —
ра́дугой су́дорог.

Как слоны́ стопудо́выми и́грами
заверша́ли побе́ду Пи́ррову,
я по́ступью ге́ния мозг твой вы́громил.
Напра́сно.
Тебя́ не вы́рву.

Ра́дуйся,
ра́дуйся,
ты докона́ла!
Тепе́рь
така́я тоска́,
что то́лько б добежа́ть до кана́ла
и го́лову су́нуть воде́ в оска́л.
Гу́бы дала́.
Как ты груба́ и́ми.
Прикосну́лся и осты́л.
Бу́дто целу́ю покая́нными губа́ми
в холо́дных ска́лах вы́сеченный монасты́рь.

Захло́пали
две́ри.
Вошёл он,
весе́льем у́лиц орошён.
Я
как на́двое расколо́лся в во́пле.
Кри́кнул ему:
«Хорошо́!
Уйду́!
Хорошо́!
Твоя́ оста́нется.
Тря́пок наше́й ей,
ро́бкие кры́лья в шелка́х зажире́ли б.
Смотри́, не уплыла́ б.

Like an apostle of old
I'll carry my love down thousands of roads.
A crown is prepared for you for the centuries,
and in the crown my words
are a rainbow of spasms.

Like the elephants
celebrated Pyrrhus' victory with thousand pound games
I'll crush your brain with the tread of genius.
No use.
I can't wrest you out.

Rejoice,
rejoice,
you've finished me off!
Now
there's such sorrow
that my only wish is to run to the canal
and stick my head into the teeth of the water.
You gave me your lips.
You're so coarse with them.
I barely touched them and my fervor died.
As if I had kissed a monastery
carved out in cold cliffs
with my repentant lips.

The doors
clapped.
He came in,
sprinkled with merriment from the streets.
I
cracked in half with a howl.
I shouted at him
"Fine!
I'll leave!
Fine!
She's yours.
Sew her some rags,
so that her timid wings can fatten in silk.
Careful that she doesn't float away.

Ка́мнем на ше́е
наве́сь жене́ жемчуга́ ожере́лий!»

Ох, эта
ночь!
Отча́янье стя́гивал ту́же и ту́же сам.
От пла́ча моего́ и хо́хота
мо́рда ко́мнаты вы́косилась у́жасом.

И виде́нием встава́л унесённый от тебя́ лик,
глаза́ми вы́зарила ты на ковре́ его́,
бу́дто вы́мечтал како́й-то но́вый Бя́лик
ослепи́тельную цари́цу Сио́на евре́ева.

В му́ке
пе́ред той, кото́рую отда́л,
коле́нопреклонённый вы́ник.
Коро́ль Альбе́рт,
все города́
отда́вший,
ря́дом со мной зада́ренный имени́нник.

Вызола́чивайтесь в со́лнце, цветы́ и тра́вы!
Весе́ньтесь, жи́зни всех стихи́й!
Я хочу́ одно́й отра́вы —
пить и пить стихи́.

Се́рдце обокра́вшая,
всего́ его́ лиши́в,
вы́мучившая ду́шу в бреду́ мою́,
прими́ мой дар, дорога́я,
бо́льше я, мо́жет быть, ничего́ не приду́маю.

В пра́здник кра́сьте сего́дняшнее число́.
Твори́сь,
распя́тью ра́вная ма́гия.
Ви́дите —
гвоздя́ми слов
приби́т к бума́ге я.

1915

Hang pearls around your wife's neck
like a stone!"

Oh, this
night!
I keep tightening and tightening my despair.
The room's ugly mug twisted in horror
from my crying and laughing.

Your countenance, sweeping away from you, arose in a vision,
you burned it onto the carpet with your eyes,
as if some new Bialik dreamed up
a dazzling Queen of Zion.

In agony
before the one I gave away,
I slumped down to my knees.
Next to me,
King Albert,
who gave away all his cities,
seems like a birthday boy, lavished with gifts.

Gild yourself in the sun, flowers and grass!
Be springlike, lives of all elements!
I only want one poison—
to drink and drink poetry.

Robbing my heart,
having deprived it of everything
torturing my soul in delirium,
accept my gift, darling,
I doubt I'll think up anything more.

Color today's date a holiday.
Come into being,
magic equal to the crucifixion.
You all can see—
I'm nailed to the paper
with words.

Флейта-позвоночник/Backbone flute

Originally titled "Verses to her," M dedicated this poem to his muse and lover Lilya Brik. This famous (and to some, notorious) couple was brought together by poetry. In the summer of 1915, M was paying court to Lilya's 17 year old younger sister Elsa. Elsa's family strongly disapproved, and rightly so—at 22 M had already had many casual affairs and was responsible for at least two unwanted pregnancies. To win them over, Elsa arranged a visit to Lilya and her husband Osip's Petersburg apartment, where M recited his just completed poem "A cloud in trousers." Her mission was more successful than she intended: M fell in love on the spot with Lilya and dedicated "Cloud" to her that very evening; Osip declared M a genius and offered to publish the poem at his own expense. M became "Uncle Volodya" to Elsa, and a second husband to Lilya, in a three-member household arrangement which lasted for 15 years.

In Lilya, M more than met his match. Lilya was many things: a free spirited-bohemian, a cultured socialite, a generous patron to aspiring artists. She was intelligent, charming, and strangely beautiful. But it seems her most exceptional quality was a supernatural power over the opposite sex, which was apparent even in her preteen years. (A characteristic story from her memoirs: at 12 or 13 she went with not one but two boys to the theater and sat between them, placing her fur muff in her lap. During the intermission she looked down to see that each of the boys, having reached into the muff to hold her hand, were now holding hands with each other.)[(1)] M's intense passion for her was never fully reciprocated—Lilya valued him more as a poet than a lover. She had many affairs with other men, but was always faithful to M in her role as first listener and auditor of new verse. For "Flute" this role was crucial—she was not only the subject of the poem, but its midwife, reviewing each new stanza in M's one-room apartment as its "non-human magic" came into being.

Prologue

All the standard elements of a religious rite are in place: an opening benediction, a lifted chalice, the pouring of wine (and body fluids!), commands to celebrate, and the physical destruction/dismemberment of the scapegoat/god. This is an invitation to the poet's Last Supper—or to a Bacchanalia, where the poet is the sacrificial bull.

(1) Ann and Samuel Chaters, *I Love, the Story of Vladimir Mayakovsky and Lili Brik* (McGraw-Hill, 1979), 9.

хранимых иконами у души в пещере/watched over by icons in the cave of my soul
Note the religious images (icons/soul/caves or catacombs) and language (compare to "Боже царя храни/God save the czar" and "Храни тебя Господь/May the Lord protect you").

подъемлю/I lift
From подымать, an archaic form of поднимать.

как чашу вина/like a cup of wine
A chalice, filled with wine and/or blood, is an attribute of both Christ and Bacchus.

не поставить ли лучше точку пули в своём конце/wouldn't it be better to punctuate my ending with a bullet
Literally, "Wouldn't it be better to place a period of a bullet at my end."

Смех из глаз в глаза лей/Pour laughter from eyes to eyes.
Из тела в тело веселье лейте/Pour merriment from body to body
Fitting commands for a Dionysian orgy.

Я сегодня буду играть на флейте/На собственном позвоночнике/Today I will play the flute, my own backbone.
It's not surprising that M rejects the lyre, the standard symbol for the poetic voice since the days of Derzhavin, in favor of the flute. He was, of course, violently opposed to tradition (suggesting, for example, that Pushkin and all the other "generals of classicism" should be attacked with cannons). What is surprising is how he twists the classical tradition here to serve his own purposes.

The lyre is the instrument of Apollo and Orpheus. It has the power to bring order from chaos: to soothe wild beasts, to control the forces of nature, and even to lead the dead out of Hades. The flute, however, is the instrument of Dionysus. It evokes passion, frenzy and madness. It is the accompaniment of elegies, dramas and sacrifices—a fitting instrument not just for Mayakovsky, but for Mayakovsky's era. M's contemporary Osip Mandelstam, for example, used images of flutes and backbones in the poem "The age," where the poet must "bind together the broken vertebrae of two centuries with his own blood," and "bind together the joints of nodular days with a flute."

1

Part one, like every section in "Flute." opens and closes with its own repeating stanza:

> I trample miles of streets with measured strides.
> Where can I go, bearing this hell?
> What kind of celestial Hoffmann
> conjured up you, cursed woman?!

These lines present the main topic for the section: the poetic impetus and the process of "cutting screams into verses." The poet's internal torment drives him through the streets of Petersburg, as he searches for relief from his "painful and clotted" thoughts. Pacing through the night, he has nightmarish fantasies about the "cursed woman" he desperately loves, and quarrels with the "celestial Hoffmann" who devised her. The impetus for the poem is suffering; the process is "trampling miles of streets with rhythmic strides."

These stanzas match M's description of the poetic process in "How to write poetry": "I walk along, waving my arms and mumbling almost wordlessly, now shortening my steps so as not to interrupt my mumbling, now mumbling more rapidly in time with my steps. And so the rhythm takes shape . . ." [(2)]

взмахами шагов/with measured strides.

Literally, "with swings of steps." Regular, repeating movement is implied—like rowing an oar. But the effect is a little strange, since "взмах/swing" is usually a movement of the arms, not the legs.

Какому небесному Гофману/What kind of celestial Hoffmann

The supernatural stories of E. T. A. Hoffmann were very popular in Russian from the 1820's, and had an deep impact on the prose of Pushkin, Gogol and Dostoevsky.

и голову вымозжу/debrain

The wonderful neologism "вымозжить" looks like a combo of "ломать голову/to rack one's brains," "выбить/to beat out," and "вымостить/to pave."

Вот я богохулил. Орал, что бога нет/I blasphemed. I shouted that there was no god

In his early poetry M truly was a prolific blasphemer. He depicts God as vicious, vengeful and ridiculous. But this may be the first time he flatly declares that "there is

(2) Carrick, 245-246.

no god." There are clear references in "Flute" to Nietzsche, and M may be identifying with Zarathustra, who famously proclaimed that "God is dead."

перед ней гора заволнуется и дрогнет/a mountain would quiver before her in excitement
Before her, a mountain will get excited and lose its stiffness/lose its cool. Not about trembling in fear, but about the power to rouse even stone—as if she's an earthquake.

Под небом в круче измученный человек одичал и вымер/under the sky on a crag an exhausted man went wild and extinct
Critics have suggested that this figure is Prometheus,(3) and there are parallels: Prometheus is chained to a mountain for disobeying Zeus, the poet is punished by god for the crime of blasphemy; Prometheus sacrifices himself to bring fire to humanity, the hero of "Flute" sacrifices himself in the act of creating poetry; and like the poet, whose skull, backbone and "blood-clot" thoughts move outside the body's boundaries, Prometheus' internals are exposed—every day a giant eagle pays a visit to tear out and eat his liver.

It's also possible that this "exhausted man" is Nietzsche's Zarathustra, who lived in the mountains for 10 years, became "extinct" (i.e. transformed himself from a man to a superman), and returned to civilization to spread the gospel that "God is dead."

метался/rushed around
To rush around uselessly and in a frenzy. Also to toss and turn in bed, unable to sleep because of sickness or delirium.

Я сам тебе, праведный, руки вымою/I myself, a righteous one, will wash your hands
Casting himself in the role of Jesus, condemned by Pontius Pilot.

(3) Max Hayward, and George Reavey, *"The Bedbug" and Selected Poetry* (Indiana University Press, 1975), 308.

2

The framing stanzas for part two are nearly identical:

> I'll light the sky,
> that's forgotten, in all the smoke, that it's blue,
> and the clouds, ragged refugees,
> in my last love,
> blazing like the burning cheeks of a consumptive.
>
> Listen, you who have forgotten that the sky is blue,
> who have bristled up
> just like beasts!
> This may be
> the last love in the world
> and it shines like the burning cheeks of a consumptive.

The intense suffering and internal pressure of part one have yielded an incredible love poem—here are the verses "cut like facets from screams." The poet has risen out of his body up to the heavens, not to be judged and tormented by god, but to "light up the sky" in a final blaze of love—a love so powerful that it has granted the poet a kind of universal consciousness. He rises above the battlefield and sees through the eyes of his enemies, he merges into the street lights of London, into the burning sand of the Sahara, into the Seine, into the "eager and naked" moon, he's a dying soldier with bullet-torn lips, he's a king, he's a slave—his love is immense and transcendent, encompassing the whole world and all of humanity.

вызарю в мою последнюю любовь/I'll illuminate the sky in my last love

The neologism "вызарить" looks like a combination of "выкрашивать/to dye or paint" and "заря/daybreak/twilight" or "зарево/glow." Other translation possibilities are "I'll paint the sky and the clouds as bright as my last love," or "I'll make the sky and the clouds shine like my last love."

рёв скопа/the roar of the crowd

Скоп is an archaic form of "скопление/a gathering."

Вылезьте из окопов/Climb out of the trenches

It's curious that all of the references to WWI, which was in full swing when M wrote this poem, are specific to the Western Front, not the Eastern. (Trench warfare never really took root in Russia). Perhaps M felt reluctant to show the war from the Russian viewpoint, since he didn't directly participate—when drafted in the fall of 1915, he made use of his connection with Gorky to win a commission as a draftsman at the Petrograd auto school.

Милые немцы!/My dear Germans!

This is a surprising way to address the enemy. M began WWI as an enthusiastic patriot, and even tried to enlist. (He was initially rejected because of his political record). But under the influence of Gorky, his attitude towards the war changed: the real enemy was not the German soldiers, but the capitalist governments which created and perpetuated the conflict, including the government of Russia.

Будешь зá море отдана/given in marriage over the sea

"За́ море" is a folksy expression, equivalent to "in a far-away land over the sea." "Отдана" is "given away," but the implication of marriage is clear.

рыжую/redhead

Lilya Brik had dark red hair, large brown eyes, a large head and "a large mouth with perfect teeth and a glowing complexion, as if she was illuminated from within." (4)

мрущим глазом быка/through the bull's dying eye.

Another key component of a Bacchanalia: the sacrificial bull.

С другим зажгёшь в огне рысаков Стрелку или Сокольники/You'll set fire to Strelka or Sokolniki with another man in the flame of carriage horses

Strelka and Sokolniki are parks in Moscow and Petersburg, popular spots for lovers to enjoy private rides in closed carriages.

запёкшееся на выдранной ядром губе/clotted with blood on my cannon torn lips

"Запекшийся/clotted" usually refers to blood.

(4) Bengt Jangfeldt, *Mayakovsky: A Poet in the Revolution,* trans by Harry D. Watson. (The University of Chocago Press, 2014), 34.

3

The bracketing stanzas of part three lay out the main theme of "Backbone Flute": bodily sacrifice as an act of creation.

> I'll forget the year, day, date.
> I'll lock myself up alone with a sheet of paper,
> Arise, non-human magic of words
> made lucid by suffering!
>
> Color today's date a holiday.
> Come into being,
> magic equal to the crucifixion
> You see—
> I'm nailed to the paper
> with words.

Part 3 is a kaleidoscope of death images. Lilya's apartment smells of funeral incense, she speaks to him coldly, she's a monastery carved into cold cliffs, she's hiding a corpse, her eyes are bottomless graves, her every muscle proclaims that her love for him is "dead! dead! dead!" No matter how brilliantly he juggles words, no matter that the "tread of his genius" is as awesome as the victory celebration of war elephants, he can't persuade her to love him. The performer crashes from the tightrope into the abyss, he cracks in half with howl, he concedes, he gives her away, he is finished off by the awful truth, which she pours on his head like lava.

With his death come multiple commands to celebrate (Rejoice! Rejoice!," "Gild yourself in the sun!," "Be springlike!," "Color today's date a holiday,"), along with the "final gift" of poetry: a rainbow of spasms in a crown of words; the paper to which poet is nailed.

нечеловечья магия/inhuman magic

An unusual form of the adjective "нечеловеческий."

только вошёл к вам/I had just come to visit you

This is "you" in plural, meaning he's visiting the Briks' apartment.

и ширился в воздухе запах ладана/and the smell of frankincense spread in the air

Frankincense is used by the Russian Orthodox Church for funeral rites.

Рада?/Happy?
Shorthand for "Are you happy to see me?"

Я отчаянье громозжу/I'll pile up despair
A typical pairing of mismatching verbs and nouns: you can heap up leaves, manure, dirt, but not grief.

не спрячешь трупа/you can't hide a corpse
The corpse being her love for him.

Страшное слово на голову лавь/Pour the awful words on my head like lava
M has turned "lava" into a verb, using the imperative form. Also, "слово" in this context is not an individual word, but rather "the news."

умерла, умерла, умерла/it's dead, it's dead, it's dead
The subject isn't named, so this could be either "she's dead" or "it's dead." Since the verbal ending is feminine, "it" would be love (любовь).

Я душу над пропастью натянул канатом/I stretched my soul over the abyss like a tightrope
Another image straight from *Thus Spoke Zarathustra*: the prophet, competing with a tightrope walker for the attention of the people gathered at the market place, declares that "Man is a rope, fastened between animal and Superman—a rope over the abyss."

любовь его износила уже/his love has worn (you) out/love has already worn him out/your love has worn him out
It's not clear who the object is here, as "его" is both a pronoun and a possessive adjective, and if "his love" is the subject, the object "you" is only implied. Either love has worn him, like a pair of shoes (износить refers to clothing or machinery, not to people), or his love has worn her out. And there's one more possibility. For the entire poem, the speaker has been addressing the world in first person singular. It's strange that he would suddenly switch to third person. For that reason, it seems that the "he" here is actually the husband. In other words: "You've already worn out his (your husband's) love, so rejuvenate yourself in *my* love, get reacquainted with the celebration of the body," etc.

Вымолоди себя/Rejuvenate yourself
сердце вызнакомь/Acquaint your heart
Back-to-back neologisms, with M's favorite verbal prefix "вы."

Как слоны . . . завершали победу Пиррову/Like elephants attained victory for Pyrrhus

The Greek general Pyrrhus used war elephants when battling the Romans.

Вошёл он, весельем улиц орошен/In came he, sprinkled with the merriment of the street

And here is Osip, the "real husband" ("настоящий муж") from part one, completely unfazed by the presence of his wife's lover. Like many modern thinkers in early 20th century Russia, the Briks strived to embody the ideas of Nikolai Chernyshevsky's novel *What Is To Be Done?,* namely women's emancipation, free love, and open marriage.

Отчаянье стягивал туже и туже сам/I myself tighten and tighten despair

As in the "heaping grief" example above, you can tighten a knot, you can tighten a noose, but you can't tighten despair.

. . .лик . . Бялик. . .царицу Сиона евреева/countenance . . .Bialik . . . queen of Jewish Zion

These lines are rather subversive: "лик/countenance" is a term reserved only for Christian deities of the Russian Orthodox variety, especially the Madonna. But Lilya was Jewish (and an adulteress and atheist to boot).

Bialik was a Jewish poet who wrote on Jewish themes.

Король Альберт/King Albert

When this poem was written, King Albert, the leader of Belgium during WW1, had been forced to surrender 90% of his country to German occupation.

Весеньтесь, жизни всех стихий!/Become springlike, lives of all elements!

Here is "springtime" in verbal format. The elements of nature (fire, water, air and earth) are commanded to "springify" themselves.

В праздник красьте сегодняшнее число/Color today's date a holiday

The final stanza of part 3 has echoes of the prologue ("Deck the night with weddings"), part one ("I, the creator of everything celebratory") and part 2 ("I'll paint the sky . . . in my last love").

гвоздями слов прибит к бумаге я/I'm nailed to the paper with nails of words The imagery of the final stanza of the poem and the opening stanza of the prologue perfectly match: the chalice/the cross; the skull overflowing with poetry/the paper to which the poet is nailed.

Ли́личка!
Вме́сто письма́

Дым таба́чный во́здух вы́ел.
Ко́мната —
глава́ в кручёныховском а́де.
Вспо́мни —
за э́тим окно́м
впервы́е
ру́ки твои́, исступлённый, гла́дил.
Сего́дня сиди́шь вот,
се́рдце в желе́зе.
День ещё —
вы́гонишь,
мо́жет быть, изруга́в.
В му́тной пере́дней до́лго не вле́зет
сло́манная дро́жью рука́ в рука́в.
Вы́бегу,
те́ло в у́лицу бро́шу я.
Ди́кий,
обезу́млюсь,
отча́яньем иссеча́сь.
Не на́до э́того,
дорога́я,
хоро́шая,
дай прости́мся сейча́с.
Всё равно́
любо́вь моя́ —
тя́жкая ги́ря ведь —
виси́т на тебе́,
куда́ ни бежа́ла б.
Дай в после́днем кри́ке вы́реветь
го́речь оби́женных жа́лоб.
Е́сли быка́ трудо́м умо́рят —
он уйдёт,
разля́жется в холо́дных во́дах.
Кро́ме любви́ твое́й,
мне
не́ту мо́ря,
а у любви́ твое́й и пла́чем не вы́молишь о́тдых.

Lilichka!
In place of a letter

Tobacco smoke corroded the air.
The room was
a chapter in Kruchenykh's hell.
Remember—
I stroked your hands
for the first time
at this window,
in a frenzy.
Today you sit there,
your heart in iron.
One more day—
you'll drive me away,
maybe after cursing me.
In the murky entryway it will take a long time
for my arm, broken from shaking, to get into the sleeve.
I'll run out,
I throw my body into the street.
Wild,
I'll drive myself out of my mind,
lacerating myself with despair.
All of this is unnecessary,
my darling,
my lovely one,
let's say goodbye right now.
All the same
my love
is a heavy weight —
it hangs on you
no matter where you run.
Let me bellow out in one last cry
the bitterness of offended grievances.
If a bull is exhausted from work—
he'll leave,
and sprawl out in cold waters.
Apart from your love,
for me
there is no sea,
but even crying and entreaties will obtain no relief from your love.

Захóчет покóя устáвший слон —
цáрственный ля́жет в опожáренном пескé.
Крóме любви́ твоéй,
мне
нéту сóлнца,
а я и не знáю, где ты и с кем.
Éсли б так поэ́та измýчила,
он
люби́мую на дéньги б и слáву вы́менял,
а мне
ни оди́н не рáдостен звон,
крóме звóна твоегó люби́мого и́мени.
И в пролёт не брóшусь,
и не вы́пью я́да,
и курóк не смогý над вискóм нажáть.
Надо мнóю,
крóме твóего взгля́да,
не влáстно лéзвие ни одногó ножá.
Зáвтра забýдешь,
что тебя́ короновáл,
что дýшу цветýщую любóвью вы́жег,
и сýетных дней взметённый карнавáл
растрéплет страни́цы мои́х кни́жек...
Слов мои́х сухи́е ли́стья ли
застáвят останови́ться,
жáдно дышá?
Дай хоть
послéдней нéжностью вы́стелить
твой уходя́щий шаг.

1916

If a worn-out elephant wants some peace —
he lies down magestically in the scorched sand.
Apart from your love,
for me
there is no sun,
but I don't know where you are or who you're with.
If you tormented a poet like that,
he
would exchange his love for money and fame,
but for me
there is not a single joyful sound
apart from your beloved name.
And no, I won't throw myself down the stairwell,
or drink poison,
and I can't press a trigger to my temple.
Apart from your gaze
no blade or knife holds power
over me.
Tomorrow you'll forget
that I crowned you,
that I burned out my blossoming soul with love,
and the whirling carnival of frivolous days
will tatter the pages of my little books . . .
Will the dry leaves of my words,
breathing avidly,
compel you to stop?
At least
with a final tenderness
allow them to cover your departing step.

Лиличка!/Lilichka!

No poet has ever depicted the anguish of a broken heart from the male perspective more powerfully than Mayakovsky. In this "final cry" to his departing beloved, he pulls out all the stops with an incredible array of rhetorical techniques:

1. metaphor: "сердце в железе/heart in iron," "любовь моя тяжкая гиря/my love is a heavy weight," "слов моих сухие листья/dry leaves of my words"
2. neologisms: "обезумлюсь/I'll drive myself out of my mind,""иссечась/having lashed myself," "опожаренный/scorched"
3. repetition: "дай простимся/Let me say goodbye," "Дай . . . выреветь/Let me roar out," "Дай хоть/Let me at least . . ."
4. parallelism: "If you wear out a bull . . . ," "If an exhausted elephant . . .," "If you treated a poet like that . . ."
5. hyperbole: an arm "broken from shaking," "not a single joyful sound apart from your name," no weapon has power "except for your gaze."
6. declamatory rhythm: "Lilichka!" is a broken mix of dactyls and trochees, with most phrases having the emphasis, like a blow, on the first syllable. The poem is bound together by the roughly alternating stresses in the ending rhymes: вы́ел/а́де, э́тим окно́м/сидишь во́т, желе́зе/не вле́зет, изруга́в/в рука́в, Вы́бегу/ бро́шу я, иссеча́сь/ сейча́с, ги́ря ведь/вы́реветь, and so forth.
7. assonance, consonance, alliteration: repeating sounds of agitation (ч/ch, з/z, х/kh, с/s, ш/sh, щ/shch) and despair (ы/i as in ill)

Дым табачный воздух выел/Tobacco smoke corroded the air.
The word выесть/выедать is used in the following contexts: acid eating through metal, moths eating holes in cloth, or scooping the yolk out of an egg. The prefix "вы" indicates thoroughness—an act done to completion. M uses it over and over here: выбегу (I run out), выреветь (to roar out), вымолить (to acquire through entreaty), выменял (exchanged); выжег (burned out), and выстелить (to pave). This repeating "вы" is another device that gives this poem such a sense of desperation and finality: The poet's last-ditch effort to stop his lover from leaving.

rova. The topic is a card game between the devil and sinners, who have wagered their souls on the outcome.

обезумлюсь, отчаяньем иссечась/I'll drive myself insane, lacerating myself with despair

Two neologisms in one line. Instead of "обезуметь," which means "to drive oneself crazy," M has taken "обезумить/to drive (someone else) crazy" and made it reflexive: "I'll drive myself out of my mind." "Иссечась," seems to mean either "having used something up by flogging oneself" or "having completely unraveled."

Дай в последнем крике выреветь/горечь обиженных жалоб/
Let me bellow out in a final cry/the bitterness of offended grievances

This couplet is remarkable for its excessiveness: a bellow within a cry amplified by the prefix "вы" (non-standard for the verb "реветь/to howl"); not just bitterness, but the very distorted "bitterness of offended grievances." (You can have an offended tone or an offended look, but not an offended complaint!)

а у любви твоей и плачем не вымолишь отдых./but crying and entreaties will obtain no relief from your love.

This is ambiguous. "Вымолить" means "to pray to the point of obtaining something," typically forgiveness from God, as in "вымолить у Бога прощение." But is he praying *to* her love for relief? Or is he begging for relief *from* her love?

опожаренном/parched

Another neoligsm, maybe a combination of "опаленный/parched" and "пожаренный/roasted."

и курок не сможет над виском нажать/and I can't press a trigger at my temple.

He actually did try to shoot himself in 1916, but the chamber was empty. Before he made a second attempt, Lilya arrived at his apartment and intervened.

взметённый карнавал/a whirling carnival

The word "взметнуть" means "to lift up abruptly or throw," with the root "мет" as in "метель" (snow storm). This, along with the dry leaves, tattered pages, and eager breathing, creates the image of a whirlwind.

Себé, люби́мому, посвящáет э́ти стрóки автóр

Четы́ре.
Тяжёлые, как удáр.
«Кéсарево кéсарю — бóгу бóгово».
А такóму,
как я,
ткну́ться кудá?
Где мне уготóвано лóгово?

Éсли бы я был
мáленький,
как океáн,-
на цы́почки волн встал,
прили́вом ласкáлся к к лунé бы.
Где люби́мую найти́ мне,
таку́ю, как и я?
Такáя не умести́лась бы в крóхотное нéбо!

О, éсли б я нищ был!
Как миллиардéр!
Что дéньги душé?
Ненасы́тный вор в ней.
Мои́х желáний разну́зданной ордé
не хвáтит зóлота всех Калифóрний.

Éсли б быть мне косноязы́чным,
как Дант
или Петрáрка!
Ду́шу к однóй зажéчь!
Стихáми велéть истлéть ей!
И словá
и любóвь моя́ —
триумфáльная áрка:
пы́шно,
бесслéдно пройду́т сквозь неé
любóвницы всех столéтий.

To his beloved self
the author dedicates these lines

Six words.
Heavy as a blow.
"Render unto Caesar . . .Render unto God. . . "
But where is
someone
like me to go?
Where is a lair prepared for me?

If I were
small,
like the ocean,
I'd rise up on the tiptoes of waves
and caress the moon
like high tide.
Where am I to find a beloved,
one like me?
She wouldn't fit in the tiny sky!

Oh, if only I were poor!
Like a billionaire!
What's money to the soul?
There's an insatiable thief inside it.
There's not enough gold in all the Californias
to satisfy the unruly horde of my desires.

If only I were incoherent,
like Dante
or Petrarch!
To set my soul on fire for one woman!
To command it to smolder with verses for her!
Both my words
and my love
are a triumphal arch:
magnificently,
without a trace, lovers of every century
will walk through it.

О, е́сли б был я
ти́хий,
как гром,-
ныл бы,
дро́жью объя́л бы земли́ одряхле́вший скит.
Я е́сли всей его́ мо́щью
вы́реву го́лос огро́мный,-
коме́ты зало́мят горя́щие ру́ки,
броса́ясь вниз с тоски́.

Я бы глаз луча́ми грыз но́чи —
о, если б был я
ту́склый, как со́лце!
О́чень мне на́до
сия́ньем мои́м пои́ть
земли́ отоща́вшее ло́нце!

Пройду́,
любо́вищу мою́ волоча́.
В како́й ночи́
бредово́й,
неду́жной
каки́ми Голиа́фами я зача́т —
тако́й большо́й
и тако́й нену́жный?

1916

Oh, if only I were
quiet,
like thunder—
I'd whine,
I'd seize the decrepit monastery of the earth with shaking—
If I roar out my huge voice
with its full power—
comets will wring their fiery hands,
throwing themselves down out of misery.

I'd gnaw the nights with the rays of my eyes—
oh, if only I were
dull like the sun!
The last thing I wanted was
to water the emaciated little bosom
of the earth with my radiance.

I'll go by,
dragging along my monstrous love.
In what delirious,
ailing
night
by what Goliaths was I conceived—
someone so big
and so unnecessary?

Себе, любимому/To his beloved self

Not satisfied to merely cast himself in the poem's starring role, the author also feels compelled to make the dedication to *himself.* You might shake your head in indignation or amusement at his self-conceit, but the initial impression quickly gives way to pathos. The dedication is an act of desperate loneliness. There's no place for the hero on earth or in heaven, and there's not even another soul to talk to: the whole poem is a monologue.

The real irony is that M was admired, respected and even loved by the other "goliaths" in Russia's poetic universe: Akhmatova, Tsvetaeva, Pasternak and Severyanin all dedicated poems to him.

Четыре/Four
There are 4 words in the phrase "Кесарево кесарю — богу богово." The traditional wording in Russian is "Кесарю кесарево, а Богу Богово" ("Render unto Caesar the things that are Caesar's, and unto God the things that are God's"), but M has taken a couple of liberties: the word order is reversed, and "god" is not capitalized.

Тяжёлые, как удар/Heavy, like a blow.
This could be a description of a sound, like a clock striking.

ткнуться куда
"Where to tuck oneself into," both figuratively and physically: not just a little corner to live in, but one's place in the world. The verb "деться" would be more standard.

Где мне уготовано логово?/Where is a lair prepared for me?
Another biblical reference: "Foxes have dens and birds have nests, but the Son of Man has no place to lay his head."

"Уготовано" has an ominous note, as in "What has fate prepared for me?"

Дант/Dante
Spelled as it's pronounced in French (the normal spelling is "Данте"), which adds a lofty (or sarcastic) note.

такой большой и такой ненужный/so big and so unnecessary
This could be M's leitmotif—so much to offer, so immensely gifted, so overflowing with poetry, but so reliably rejected by the petty crowd, by his indifferent lover, and by his misguided peers.

M literally was a kind of goliath—about 6'3", loud, and ostentatious. From Lilya's memoirs:

> "I saw right away that Volodya was a poet of genius, but I didn't like him. I didn't like loud-mouthed people—outwardly loud-mouthed. I didn't like the fact that he was so big that people turned to look at him in the street, I didn't like the fact that he listened to his own voice, I didn't even like his name—Mayakovsky—so noisy and so like a pseudonym, a vulgar one at that. [(1)]

(1) Jangfeldt, 80.

Ле́вый марш

Развора́чивайтесь в ма́рше!
Слове́сной не ме́сто кля́узе.
Ти́ше, ора́торы!
Ва́ше
сло́во,
това́рищ ма́узер.
Дово́льно жить зако́ном,
да́нным Ада́мом и Е́вой.
Кля́чу исто́рии заго́ним.
Ле́вой!
Ле́вой!
Ле́вой!

Эй, синеблу́зые!
Ре́йте!
За океа́ны!
И́ли
у бронено́сцев на ре́йде
сту́плены о́стрые ки́ли?!
Пусть,
оска́лясь коро́ной,
вздыма́ет брита́нский лев вой.
Комму́не не быть покорённой.
Ле́вой!
Ле́вой!
Ле́вой!

Там
за гора́ми го́ря
со́лнечный край непоча́тый.
За го́лод
за мо́ра мо́ре
шаг миллио́нный печа́тай!
Пусть ба́ндой окру́жат на́нятой,
стально́й излива́ются ле́евой,-
Росси́и не быть под Анта́нтой.
Ле́вой!
Ле́вой!
Ле́вой!

Left march

Swing out in formation!
This is no place for squabbles.
Be quiet, orators!
Your
word,
comrade Mauser.
Enough living by laws
given by Adam and Eve.
We'll drive the nag of history to exhaustion.
Left!
Left!
Left!

Hey, blue-blouses!
Sail!
Over the oceans!
Or have the sharp keels
of the battle ships gotten dull
in the port?!
Let
the British lion raise a howl
baring its crown.
The commune won't be conquered.
Left!
Left!
Left!

There,
beyond mountains of grief,
there's a sunny abundance.
Because of hunger
because of the sea of pestilence
imprint the millionth step!
Let a hired gang surround us,
let them flow out in a steely stream,
Russia will not be under the Entente.
Left!
Left!
Left!

Глаз ли помéркнет óрлий?
В стáрое стáнем ли пя́литься?
Крепи́
у ми́ра на гóрле
пролетариáта пáльцы!
Грýдью вперёд брáвой!
Флáгами нéбо оклéивай!
Кто там шагáет прáвой?
Лéвой!
Лéвой!
Лéвой!

1920

Will the eagle's eye grow dim?
Will we stare into the past?
Tighten
proletarian fingers
around the world's throat!
Brave chests forward!
Paper the sky with flags!
Who there is marching right?
Left!
Left!
Left!

Левый марш/Left march

Anatoly Lunacharsky, the first Soviet Commissar of Education, described M as a self-obsessed adolescent, "whining on account of unsuccessful love affairs and the lack of recognition of his youthful genius from the cruel crowd."(1) But in "Left march," M has adopted a dramatically different persona: poet of the revolution.

The new Soviet Republic, barely a year old, needed his service, and "Left march" was written on commission:

> "I received a phone call from the Naval Guard Headquarters and was ordered to go and read them some poetry, and so while in the cab I wrote 'Left march.' Of course, some of the stanzas had been ready before, and all I had to do was link up the ones addressed to sailors."(2)

With the revolution, it seemed that M had finally found his "уготованное логово" in the world—"a place prepared for me." The Republic appreciated him, needed him, and directed his enormous talent towards a cause: the building of socialism.

Разворачивайтесь в марше/swing out into a march
A sailor might be confused by this order, since it's not a legitimate drill command. The immediate associations are "разворачивать веер/unfold a fan" and "сделать разворот/make a u-turn." The image is of marching columns pivoting and unfolding like a fan.

синеблузые/blue shirts
"Синеблузник" is someone who wears a blue shirt; a worker. "Синяя блуза/The Blue Blouse" was a popular Soviet theater collective in the '20s, whose mission was to deliver news and propaganda to the masses. M has created his own variation: "blue-bloused people."

солнечный край непочатый/an untouched sunny land
A mangling of two set phrases, "край непочатый/an untouched abundance" and "солнечный край/sunlit land."

---

(1) Bykov, 367.

(2) Carrick, 267. From *Address to the Krasnaya Presnya Komsomol Club at an Evening Dedicated to Twenty Years of Work.*

оскалясь короной/baring its crown

In a threatening gesture, the lion from the UK royal coat of arms bares its crown (as opposed to its teeth) .

За голод за мора море/For hunger for pestilences

"За" as in "a response to," or as "an answer to."

стальной изливаются леевой/pours out in a steely stream

M has formed the noun "леева" from the verb "лить/to pour."

Антантой/Triple Entente

The Triple Entente was the alliance of Russia, France and Great Britain before WW1. After the Soviet Republic withdrew from the war, its former allies Britain, France and America intervened in the Russian Civil War to fight on the side of the Whites against the Bolsheviks.

Кто там шагает правой? Левой! Левой! Левой!/Who there is marching right? Left! Left! Left!

M was left handed, and according to the conventions of the time, was forced to learn to write and draw with his right hand. With the revolution it seemed that convention was now on his side. This poem is not just a call to fight for the revolution; it's a manifestation of M's "leftness," as the critic Dmitri Bykov describes below:

> "Like all lefthanders, he felt different than others, and was therefore by default sympathetic to all things 'left,' as opposed to 'right.' The famous, reliably crowd-pleasing 'Left March' is a manifest of his leftism, his left-handedness, his 'leftness' . . . in essence, all leftists, unable to function like normal humans, have 'left-handed lives,' and for that reason want to remake the world."(3)

---

(3) Bykov, 367

Хоро́шее отноше́ние к лошадя́м

Би́ли копы́та,
Пе́ли бу́дто:
— Гриб.
Грабь.
Гроб.
Груб.—
Ве́тром опи́та,
льдом обу́та
у́лица скользи́ла.
Ло́шадь на круп
гро́хнулась,
и сра́зу
за зева́кой зева́ка,
штаны́ прише́дшие Кузне́цким клёшить,
сгру́дились,
смех зазвене́л и зазвя́кал:
— Ло́шадь упа́ла! —
— Упа́ла ло́шадь! —
Смея́лся Кузне́цкий.
Лишь оди́н я
го́лос свой не вме́шивал в вой ему́.
Подошёл
и ви́жу
глаза́ лошади́ные...

У́лица опроки́нулась,
течёт по-сво́ему...
Подошёл и ви́жу —
За ка́плищей ка́плища
по мо́рде ка́тится,
пря́чется в ше́рсти...

И кака́я-то о́бщая
звери́ная тоска́
плеща́ вы́лилась из меня́
и расплыла́сь в ше́лесте.
«Ло́шадь, не на́до.
Ло́шадь, слу́шайте —
чего́ вы ду́маете, что вы их пло́ше?

Being good to horses

Hooves were beating,
As if singing:
"Grib,
Grab.
Grob.
Grub."
Slaked with the wind,
shoed in ice,
the street slid.
A horse tumbled
onto its rear,
and immediately
one gawker after another
having arrived to flare their pants along Kuznetsky,
clustered around,
laughter rang out and jingled:
"A horse fell!"
"A horse fell down!"
laughed Kuznetsky.
I was the only one
who didn't mix his voice in with the street's howling.
I walk over—
and see
the horse's eyes . . .

The street toppled over,
and flows off on its own way . . .
I walk over and see—
one big drop after another
streaming down her muzzle
and hiding in her hair.

And a sort of mutual
animal sadness
poured out of me, splashing,
and spread into the rustling of the street.
"Horse, don't.
Horse, listen—
why would you think you're worse than them?

Де́точка,
все мы немно́жко ло́шади,
ка́ждый из нас по-сво́ему ло́шадь.»
Мо́жет быть,
— ста́рая —
и не нужда́лась в ня́ньке,
мо́жет быть, и мысль ей моя́ каза́лась пошла́,
то́лько
ло́шадь
рвану́лась,
вста́ла на но́ги,
ржану́ла
и пошла́.
Хвосто́м пома́хивала.
Ры́жий ребёнок.
Пришла́ весёлая,
ста́ла в сто́йло.
И всё ей каза́лось –
она́ жеребёнок,
и сто́ило жить,
и рабо́тать сто́ило.

1918

My poor dear,
all of us are horses, a little bit,
every one of us is a horse in his own way."
Maybe
she was old
and didn't need a nanny,
maybe my thought seemed vulgar to her,
only
the horse
lunged,
stood up,
gave a neigh,
and walked off.
She was swinging her tail.
A red-haired child.
She arrived cheerful,
and stood in the stall.
And it seemed to her
that she was a foal,
and it was worth it to live,
and it was worth it to work.

Хорошее отношение к лошадям/Being good to horses

Being *bad* to horses is a familiar motif in Russian literature. The jeering crowd, the horse's sorrowful eyes, the empathetic witness—all of this is very close to Raskolnikov's famous dream in *Crime and Punishment*, where a boy watches in horror as a peasant beats his mare to death, to the amusement of his drunken friends. There's an even earlier model with all the same elements—"Being good" might be a happy remake of a gruesome passage from N. Nekrasov's "Till twilight:"[(1)]

Under the man's cruel hand,
Barely alive, horribly emaciated,
An old nag is straining
Dragging a load that's beyond her strength.
She staggered and stopped.
"Well!" the driver grabbed a piece of wood
(The whip didn't seem adequate)—
And beat her, and beat her again and again!
Her legs somehow moved apart,
Steaming, settling back,
The horse gave a deep sigh
And looked over (the way humans do,
Submitting to an unjustified attack).
And again, along the back, along the sides,
And running in front, along her shoulders,
And along her crying tender eyes!
All in vain. The nag stood there,
Her hide striped from the whip.
Only answering each blow
With an even movement of her tail.
This amused the idle crowd,
And each put in a word.
I was angry and thought dejectedly,
"Shouldn't I intercede for her?
Sympathy is the fashion these days.
I'm not against helping you.
Humble victim of the people,
But we can't even help ourselves!"
And the driver's efforts weren't in vain—
At last he achieved his goal!
But the final scene was
A revolting spectacle for the eyes.
The horse suddenly exerted herself—
and set off
Somehow moving sideways,
with nervous haste,
And with each step the driver,
In gratitude for these efforts,
Rewarded her with a flurry of blows
Running unburdened alongside her.

Гриб. Грабь. Гроб. Груб./Grib. Grab. Grob. Grub.

Not only the sounds of hooves beating along the icy road, but individual words: Mushroom. Plunder (imperative familiar). Coffin. Crude (short form masculine adjective).[(2)]

(1) For a detailed discussion on the Nekrasov/Mayakovsky connection, see Bykov, 446-448.

(2) Edward J. Brown, *Mayakovsky: A Poet in the Revolution* (Princeton University Press, 1973), 187.

штаны пришедшие Кузнецким клёшить/to flare their pants along Kuznetsky

M. has turned the noun "клеш/flare" (as in "расклешенные штаны/bell-bottomed pants") into a verb. Kuznetsky Most, a fashionable street in central Moscow, is in the instrumental case, meaning either "along Kuznetsky" or "with Kuznetsky," as if the idlers are somehow using the street to flare their pants.

голос свой не вмешивал в вой ему/I didn't mix my voice into its howl

The dative case indicates the possessive: "вой ему/its howl."

Подошёл и вижу/I walk up and see

A good example of the fluidity of verb tense in Russian—"подошёл" is past perfective; "вижу" is present. A literal translation doesn't work well in English: "I walked up and see."

Улица опрокинулась/The street rolled over

A wonderful example of personification—drunk with wind and shoed in ice, the street slips, knocks over a horse, stops to laugh, rolls itself over and then goes about its business.

чего вы думаете, что вы сих плоше/why do you think you're worse

M is addressing the horse respectfully, as "вы," which is funny and touching, since animals are always addressed in the familiar as "ты."

"Плоше" is a comparitive form of "плохо/bad."

ржанула/whinnied

M has invented a perfective form of the "ржать/to neigh": to give a neigh.

Необыча́йное приключе́ние, бы́вшее с Влади́миром Маяко́вским ле́том на да́че

(Пу́шкино, Аку́лова гора́, да́ча Румя́нцева,
27 вёрст по Яросла́вской жел. дор.)

В сто со́рок солнц зака́т пыла́л,
в ию́ль кати́лось ле́то,
была́ жара́,
жара́ плыла́ —
на да́че бы́ло э́то.
Приго́рок Пу́шкино горби́л
Аку́ловой горо́ю,
а низ горы́ —
дере́вней был,
криви́лся крыш коро́ю.
А за дере́внею —
дыра́,
и в ту дыру́, наве́рно,
спуска́лось со́лнце ка́ждый раз,
ме́дленно и ве́рно.
А за́втра
сно́ва
мир зали́ть
встава́ло со́лнце а́ло.
И день за днём
ужа́сно злить
меня́
вот э́то
ста́ло.
И так одна́жды разозля́сь,
что в стра́хе всё побле́кло,
в упо́р я кри́кнул со́лнцу:
«Слазь!
дово́льно шля́ться в пе́кло!»
Я кри́кнул со́лнцу:
«Дармое́д!
зане́жен в облака́ ты,
а тут — не знай ни зим, ни лет,
сиди́, рису́й плака́ты! »
Я кри́кнул со́лнцу:

An astonishing adventure had by Vladimir Mayakovsky in summer at the dacha

(Pushkino, Akulova Hill, Rumyantsev's dacha,
18 miles by rail on the Yaroslavsky line)

The sunset blazed like a hundred suns,
summer rolled into July,
the weather was hot,
the heat was floating–
this was in the country.
Pushkino knoll bent over into
Akulova Hill,
And at the foot of the hill
there was a village,
crooked with bark roofs.
And behind the village—
was a hole,
and every time, no doubt,
the sun descended into that hole,
slowly and steadily.
And tomorrow
again
the sun would arise, crimson,
to flood the world.
And day after day
this
began
to infuriate
me.
And so one time getting so enraged,
that everything paled in terror,
I yelled right at the sun:
"Climb down!
that's enough traipsing around in the inferno!"
I yelled at the sun:
You free-loader!
You're wallowing in the clouds,
And here—winter or summer,
I have to sit and make posters!"
I yelled at the sun:

«Погоди́!
послу́шай, златоло́бо,
чем так,
без де́ла заходи́ть,
ко мне
на чай зашло́ бы!»
Что я наде́лал!
Я поги́б!
Ко мне,
по до́брой во́ле,
само́,
раски́нув луч-шаги́,
шага́ет со́лнце в по́ле.
Хочу́ испу́г не показа́ть —
и ретиру́юсь за́дом.
Уже́ в саду́ его́ глаза́.
Уже́ прохо́дит са́дом.
В око́шки,
в две́ри,
в щель войдя́,
вали́лась со́лнца ма́сса,
ввали́лось;
дух переведя́,
заговори́ло ба́сом:
«Гоню́ обра́тно я огни́
впервы́е с сотворе́нья.
Ты звал меня́?
Чай гони́,
гони́, поэ́т, варе́нье!»
Слеза́ из глаз у самого́ —
жара́ с ума́ своди́ла,
но я ему́ —
на самова́р:
«Ну что ж,
сади́сь, свети́ло!»
Чёрт дёрнул дёрзости мои́
ора́ть ему́, —
сконфу́жен,
я сел на уголо́к скамьи́,
бою́сь — не вы́шло б ху́же!
Но стра́нная из со́лнца ясь

"Hold on!
listen, goldy-brow,
instead of
dropping down for no good reason,
why not drop by
for tea!"
What have I done!
I'm doomed!!
Of his own free will,
the sun himself,
stretching out his ray-steps
is striding through the field
straight towards me.
I don't want to show any fear,
and retreat, rear end first.
His eyes are already in the garden.
He's passing through the garden already.
The sun's mass
spilled through the windows,
the doors,
the cracks,
the sun tumbled in;
drawing a breath,
he began speaking in a bass:
"I'm holding back my lights
for the first time since creation.
You invited me?
Get out the tea,
poet, get out the jam!"
I'm tearing up from the heat—
it was driving me mad,
but I motioned him
towards the samovar:
"Well, OK,
have a seat, your luminescence!"
The devil must have given me the impudence
to shout at him—
embarrassed,
I sat down on the corner of the bench,
worried that things could get worse!
But a strange brightness

струи́лась, —
и степе́нность
забы́в,
сижу́, разговоря́сь
с свети́лом постепе́нно.
Про то,
про э́то говорю́,
что-де зае́ла Ро́ста,
а со́лнце:
«Ла́дно,
не горю́й,
смотри́ на ве́щи про́сто!
А мне, ты ду́маешь,
свети́ть
легко́?
— Поди́, попро́буй! —
А вот идёшь —
взяло́сь идти́,
идёшь — и свети́шь в о́ба!»
Болта́ли так до темноты́ —
до бы́вшей но́чи то есть.
Кака́я тьма уж тут?
На «ты»
мы с ним, совсе́м осво́ясь.
И ско́ро,
дру́жбы не тая́,
бью по плечу́ его́ я.
А со́лнце то́же:
«Ты да я,
нас, това́рищ, дво́е!
Пойдём, поэ́т,
взори́м,
вспоём
у ми́ра в се́ром хла́ме.
Я бу́ду со́лнце лить своё,
а ты — своё,
стиха́ми».
Стена́ тене́й,
ноче́й тюрьма́
под солнц двуство́лкой па́ла.
Стихо́в и све́та кутерьма́ —

streamed out of the sun,
and forgetting
all formality,
I sit, getting into a conversation
with the luminary little by little.
I talk about this
about that,
how Rosta was tormenting me,
and the sun:
"All right,
don't feel so sad,
look at things simply!
Do you think
it's easy for me
to shine?
Just try!
But you carry on,
since you've taken it on,
you go along and shine your eyes out!"
We jabbered like that until dark—
that is, until what used to be night.
How could it possibly be dark here?
We're on a first-name basis
completely at ease with each other.
And soon,
not hiding my friendly feelings,
I'm clapping him on the shoulder.
And the sun too:
"You and I,
the two of us, comrade, are a pair!
Let's go, poet,
let's shine forth,
let's burst out singing
in the grey rubbish of the world.
I'll pour out mine in sunshine
and you—pour out yours
in verse."
The wall of shadows,
the prison of nights,
fell under the sun's double barreled gun.
A commotion of poetry and light—

сия́й во что попа́ло!
Уста́нет то,
и хо́чет ночь
приле́чь,
тупа́я со́нница.
Вдруг — я
во всю света́ю мочь —
и сно́ва день трезво́нится.
Свети́ть всегда́,
свети́ть везде́,
до дней после́дних до́нца,
свети́ть —
и никаки́х гвозде́й!
Вот ло́зунг мой —
и со́лнца!

1920

shine on no matter comes along!
The night might get tired
and want
to lie down,
the dim-witted sleepyhead.
All of the sudden, I
shine with all my might,
and daytime rings out again.
Shine forever,
shine everywhere,
until the end of the end of days,
shine—
and that’s all there is to it!
That’s my motto—
and the sun’s!

Необычайное приключение/An astonishing adventure

When M wrote this poem in the summer of 1920, he had been working for the state news agency ROSTA for nearly a year, cranking out propaganda posters on topics of politics, war, hygiene and social behavior. The ROSTA posters were an updated, Soviet version of the peasant *lubok*—traditional woodcut prints with religious and folk themes. The posters laid out a simple story, usually in 4 panels, like a comic strip. The accompanying political messages were couched in folk format, with simple rhymes, and references to popular songs, sayings and fairy tales.

The ROSTA influence is very apparent in "An astonishing adventure": the language is folksy, the meter is simple (iambic tetrameter) and the plot has the universal elements of a fairy tale. The poem can be laid out as a 5-panel propaganda poster:(1)

1. Setting: In a village outside of Moscow, the poet is spending a hot summer at the dacha.
2. Conflict: Irritated by the relentless heat, the poet starts haranguing the sun, and sarcastically invites him over for tea.
3. Confrontation: To the poet's surprise and horror, the sun actually drops by the dacha for a visit.
4. Victory: After an awkward start, the sun and the poet become engrossed in a long conversation, and their initial antagonism resolves in friendship.
5. Moral: The poet and the sun now unite as a "double-barreled shotgun" to brighten the world with light and poetry. The poem ends with a resounding command to "Shine forever! Shine everywhere! Shine on no matter what!" In other words, "Workers! Don't be discouraged! Continue to do your part for socialism!"

Пушкино/Pushkino

The little village of "Pushkino" is the first of many Pushkin references.(2) Pushkin is "the sun of Russian poetry." The poem is written entirely in iambic tetrameter, Pushkin's preferred meter. The motif of inviting the sun for tea is also straight from Pushkin: in the drama *The Stone Guest*, Don Juan invites the statue of "the Com-

(1) On the occasion of M's 1925 tour in America, David Burliuk even illustrated a special edition of the poem with woodcuts, in *lubok* style.

(2) See Michael Wachtel, *The Development of Russian Verse* (Cambridge University Press, 1998), 12-14.

mander" to come witness the seduction of his widow, and is also horrified when his guest actually arrives. M uses this theme again in "Jubilee," when he casually invites Puskin's statue to step down from its pedestal for a stroll and a chat (and momentarily slips into iambs: "Я даже ямбом подсюсюкнул, чтоб только быть приятней вам/I'll even lisp in iambs, if that'll make you happy").

Every Russian poet must come to terms with Pushkin, and "Adventure" can be viewed as this rite of passage for M. Before this poem, M only referred to Pushkin with adolescent contempt, saying that he should be thrown off the ship of modernity, or, as in "Too early to rejoice," simply executed. Post-revolution Mayakovsky has found his place in the world, selflessly serving the new Soviet Republic as "poet of the revolution," and is now mature and confident enough to make his peace with "the sun" of Russian poetry.

Dmitri Bykov offers a different interpretation. Looking at "Jubilee," "Vladimir Ilyich Lenin," and "Adventure" as a group, Bykov argues that this is the poet's attempt to assert his own legitimacy over the heads of his contemporaries—that M is a "modern goliath" who can expect approval, protection and the summons for further creative work only from those who are as great as he is (Pushkin, Lenin, and the sun).(3)

Акулова гора, дача Румянцева/Rumyatsev's dacha
M. spent every summer at the same rented country house in Pushkino, along with the Briks and various friends. This is a good setting for an encounter with a magical creature: a cottage in a far and distant land, 18 miles from Moscow!

"Акулова гора/Shark mountain," a hill in the countryside of Pushkino, is nowhere near any sharks (Pushkino is 400 miles from the sea) and it's also nowhere near the height of an actual mountain.

была жара, жара плыла/there was heat, the heat swam
The poem opens with something very close to "жил был," or "once upon a time."

деревней/деревнею/the village
Here are two different instrumental versions of "деревня." The second version is more colloquial, and is also convenient for the rhyme (горою/деревнею).

я крикнул солнцу/I yelled to the sun
"я крикнул солнцу" is repeated 3 times, a triple invocation typical of fairy tales.

(3) Bykov, 517-8.

Слазь! Довольно шляться в пекло!/Climb down! That's enough traipsing around!

Two very folksy phrases. Instead of "Слазь," the normal command would be "Слезай!" Other examples of very informal language: "Ну что ж, садись, светило/Well whatever, have a seat, your luminosity" "Про то, про это говорю, что-де заела Роста/I talk about this and that, how I was sick of Rosta."

занежен в облака ты/you're overpampered in the clouds

"Занежен" is Mayakovky's invention. The prefix "за" indicates that the action has been done to excess: spoiled by too much loafing.

сиди, рисуй плакаты!/you sit and make posters!

Though this is an imperative, it's an emphatic way of saying "I have to." This construction is often used in proverbs.

без дела заходить/drop down for no good reason

A pun, as the the verb заходить means "the sun sets" (as in the famous folk song "Солнце всходит и заходит/The sun rises and sets"), and also "to drop by" for a visit.

Уже проходит садом/already passing through the garden

The instrumental case gives this the meaning "through the garden."

Гоню обратно я огни . . . Чаи гони, гони, поэт, варенье!/I'm driving back the fires . . . fetch the tea and jam, poet!

The verb гнать is used three times in succession, each time with a different meaning —1. drive back the fires, as if herding a flock of animals, 2. a colloquial expression meaning to drink cup after cup of tea (notice the plural of чай), and 3. and to turn out/hand over, as in "*Гони* все деньги, сейчас же!" "All the money, now!"

The sun's triple repetition of "гнать" is also a matching response to the poet's triple challenge to the sun ("я крикнул солнцу . . . " "я крикнул солнцу . . ." "я крикнул солнцу . . .").

Слеза из глаз/a tear from my eyes

Very folksy usage: "tear" is in the singular, but the meaning is plural.

Чёрт дёрнул дерзости мои орать ему/The devil made me yell my impudencies at him.

"The verb "дерзить" ("to be impertinent') is not used with first person, so a paraphrase ("говорю дерзости/I'm speaking impudencies") is needed.

ясь/brightness

A folksy rendition, from the verb "яснеть/become clear."

что-де заела Роста/I said I was sick of Rosta

"Де," like "мол" indicates that direct speech is being quoted.

взорим, вспоём/we'll shine forth, we'll burst into song

"Взорить" is an old and rare variation of "взирать/to gaze," but here it is probably a combination of "взирать" and "заря/dawn." The prefix "вз/вс" combined with "петь/to sing" is also unorthodox. The literal meaning would be "to sing upwards."

трезвонится/ring out

M has a fondness not only for non-orthodox prefixes, but also for the reflexive suffix "ся." Here he has added it onto to the intransitive verb "трезвонить/to ring," making it "to thoroughly ring itself out."

Светить всегда, светить везде/Shine forever, shine everywhere

Like "Being good to horses," this "adventure" ends in rousing, life affirming slogan.

до дней последних донца/To the bottom of the last days

A play on the set expression "до дна/to the dregs." Донец is a diminutive of "дно/bottom."

и никаких гвоздей/no matter what

A set phrase, which literally means "no nails whatsoever."

Люблю́

Обыкнове́нно так

Любо́вь любо́му рождённому да́дена,—
но ме́жду служб,
дохо́дов
и про́чего
со дня на день
очерствева́ет серде́чная по́чва.
На се́рдце те́ло наде́то,
на те́ло — руба́ха.
Но и э́того ма́ло!
Оди́н —
идио́т! —
манже́ты наде́лал
и гру́ди стал залива́ть крахма́лом.
Под ста́рость спохва́тятся.
Же́нщина ма́жется.
Мужчи́на по Мю́ллеру ме́льницей ма́шется.
Но по́здно.
Морщи́нами мно́жится ко́жица.
Любо́вь поцветёт,
поцветёт —
и скуко́жится.

I love

That's how it goes

Love is granted to anyone who's born—
but with jobs,
earnings,
and so forth
from day to day
the heart's soil hardens.
A body is put on the heart,
on the body—a shirt.
But even that's not enough!
One guy—
the idiot!—
made a lot of cuffs
and began to douse
shirtfronts with starch.
Towards old age they'll suddenly realize what's happening.
A woman puts makeup on herself.
A man waves his arms like windmills according to Müller.
But it's too late.
Wrinkles proliferate on the skin.
Love will bloom for a moment,
bloom—
and wither.

Мальчи́шкой

Я в ме́ру любо́вью был ода́ренный.
Но с де́тства
людьё
труда́ми муштро́вано.
А я —
убёг на бе́рег Рио́на
и шля́лся,
ни чёрта не делая ро́вно.
Серди́лась ма́ма:
«Мальчи́шка парши́вый!»
Грози́лся папа́ша по́ясом вы́стегать.
А я,
разживя́сь трёхрублёвкой фальши́вой,
игра́л с солдатьём под забо́ром в «три ли́стика».
Без гру́за руба́х,
без башма́чного гру́за
жа́рился в кутаисском зно́е.
Вора́чивал со́лнцу то спи́ну,
то пу́зо —
пока́ под ло́жечкой не зано́ет.
Диви́лось со́лнце:
«Чуть ви́ден ве́сь-то!
А то́же —
с серде́чком.
Стара́ется ма́лым!
Отку́да
в э́том
в арши́не
ме́сто —
и мне,
и реке́,
и стовёрстым ска́лам?!»

As a boy

I was moderately gifted with love.
But from childhood
the human herd
is drilled by labors.
But I
ran off to the bank of the Rioni
and loafed around,
not doing a damn thing.
Mama got angry:
"You lousy kid!"
Pops threatened to whip me with a belt.
But I
got hold of a fake 3-rouble note,
and played "three leaves" next to the fence with some soldiers.
Without the burden of a shirt,
or the burden of shoes
I roasted myself in the Kutaisi heat.
I would turn my back to the sun,
and then my belly—
until the pit of my stomach started to ache.
The sun marveled:
"You can barely see him!
And yet—
he's got a heart.
He's doing his best with that little thing!
Where
in this
couple of feet
is there room—
for me,
and for the river,
and for the hundred mile cliffs?

Ю́ношей

Ю́ношеству заня́тий ма́сса.
Грамма́тикам у́чим ду́рней и дур мы.
Меня́ ж
из 5-го вы́шибли кла́сса.
Пошли́ швыря́ть в моско́вские тю́рьмы.
В ва́шем
кварти́рном
ма́леньком ми́рике
для спа́лен расту́т кучеря́вые ли́рики.
Что вы́ищешь в э́тих боло́ночьих ли́риках?!
Меня́ вот
люби́ть
учи́ли
в Буты́рках.
Что мне тоска́ о Було́нском ле́се?!
Что мне вздох от ви́дов на мо́ре?!
Я вот
в «Бюро́ похоро́нных проце́ссий»
влюби́лся
в глазо́к 103-й ка́меры.
Глядя́т ежедне́вное со́лнце,
зазна́ются.
«Чего́, мол, сто́ют лучёнышки э́ти?»
А я
за стенно́го
за жёлтого за́йца
о́тдал тогда́ бы — всё на све́те.

As a youth

Young people are given loads of lessons.
We teach grammars to male and female fools.
As for me,
they kicked me out of 5th grade,
and began tossing me into the Moscow prisons.
In your
little apartment world
lyric poets with curly locks grow up for bedrooms.
What can you ever find in these lapdog poets?!
As for me,
I was taught
to love
in Butyrka.
What do I care about yearning for the Bois de Boulogne?!
What do I care about sighs over seascapes?!
Me,
I fell in love
with the Funeral Home
through the peephole of cell 103.
They look at the everyday sun
and get presumptuous.
"What," they say, "are these little rays worth?"
But I
would have given everything on earth back then
for a spot of sunlight
along the wall.

Мой университе́т

Францу́зский зна́ете.
Де́лите.
Мно́жите.
Склоня́ете чу́дно.
Ну и склоня́йте!
Скажи́те —
а с до́мом спе́ться
мо́жете?
Язы́к трамва́йский вы понима́ете?
Птене́ц челове́чий
чуть то́лько вы́велся —
за кни́жки руко́й,
за тетра́дные де́сти.
А я обуча́лся а́збуке с вы́весок,
листа́я страни́цы желе́за и же́сти.
Зе́млю возьму́т,
обкорна́в,
ободра́в её,—
у́чат.
И вся она́ — с кро́хотный гло́бус.
А я
бока́ми учи́л геогра́фию,—
неда́ром же
на́земь
ночёвкой хло́паюсь!
Мутя́т Илова́йских больны́е вопро́сы:
— Была́ ль рыжа́ борода́ Барбаро́ссы? —
Пуска́й!
Не копа́юсь в пропы́ленном вздо́ре я —
люба́я в Москве́ мне изве́стна исто́рия!
Беру́т Добролю́бова (чтоб зло ненави́деть), —
фами́лья ж про́тив,
скули́т родова́я.
Я
жи́рных
с де́тства привы́к ненави́деть,
всегда́ себя́
за обе́д продава́я.
Нау́чатся,

My university

You know French.
You divide.
You multiply.
You decline wonderfully.
Well decline then!
Tell me—
can you
pal around with a building?
Do you understand the language of streetcars?
A human baby bird
barely hatched
reaches for a booklet,
for a sheaf of notebook paper.
But I learned the alphabet from street signs,
turning over pages of iron and tin.
They take the earth,
having whittled it down,
peeled it,
and teach it.
And all of it—the size of a tiny globe.
But I
studied geography with the sides of my body—
it's not for nothing
that I flop down on the ground
for the night.
Painful questions torment the Ilovaiskis
"Was Barbarossa's beard red?"
Fine!
I won't dig into dusty rubbish—
every event in Moscow is known to me!
They take Dobrolyubov (to learn to hate evil),
the ancestral name itself
whines in opposition.
I've
hated the fat and wealthy
since childhood,
always
selling myself for a meal.
They'll complete their education,

ся́дут —
чтоб нра́виться да́ме,
мысли́шки звя́кают лбёнками ме́дненькими.
А я
говори́л
с одни́ми дома́ми.
Одни́ водока́чки мне собесе́дниками.
Окно́м слуховы́м внима́тельно слу́шая,
лови́ли кры́ши — что бро́шу в у́ши я.
А по́сле
о но́чи
и друг о дру́ге
треща́ли,
язы́к воро́чая — флю́гер.

sit down—
wanting to appeal to a lady,
their little thoughts jingle in brass foreheads.
But I
only
talked to buildings.
I only had conversations with water towers.
Listening attentively with their dormer windows
the rooftops tried to catch anything I threw in their ears.
And afterwards
they jabbered
about the night
and about each other
wagging their weathervane tongues.

Взро́слое

У взро́слых дела́.
В рубля́х карма́ны.
Люби́ть?
Пожа́луйста!
Ру́бликов за́ сто.
А я,
бездо́мный,
ручи́ща
в рва́ный
в карма́н засу́нул
и шля́лся, глаза́стый.
Ночь.
Надева́ете лу́чшее пла́тье.
Душо́й отдыха́ете на жёнах, на вдо́вах.
Меня́
Москва́ души́ла в объя́тьях
кольцо́м свои́х бесконе́чных Садо́вых.
В сердца́,
в часи́шки
любо́вницы ти́кают.
В восто́рге партнёры любо́вного ло́жа.
Столи́ц сердцеби́ение ди́кое
лови́л я,
Страстно́ю пло́щадью лёжа.
Враспа́шку —
се́рдце почти́ что сна́ру́жи —
себя́ открыва́ю и со́лнцу и лу́же.
Входи́те страстя́ми!
Любо́вями вла́зьте!
Отны́не я се́рдцем пра́вить не вла́стен.
У про́чих зна́ю се́рдца дом я.
Оно́ в груди́ — любо́му изве́стно!
На мне ж
с ума́ сошла́ анато́мия.
Сплошно́е се́рдце —
гуди́т повсеме́стно.
О, ско́лько их,
одни́х то́лько вёсен,
за 20 лет в распалённого вва́лено!

Adult

Adults have occupations.
Pockets stuffed with rubles.
Love?
Be my guest!
For a mere hundred rubles.
But I,
homeless,
thrust my paw
into a torn
pocket
and loafed around, wide-eyed.
Night.
Put on your best clothes.
Find consolation with wives and widows.
Moscow
smothered me in embraces
with the ring of its endless Sadovayas.
Mistresses tick
into hearts,
into little watches.
Partners on love's bed are in ecstasy.
I heard
the wild heart palpitations of capitals,
lying on Strastnaya square.
Unbuttoned,
my heart nearly on the outside—
opening myself up to sun and puddle.
Come in with your passions!
Climb in with your loves!
I'm no longer capable of ruling my heart.
I know where the heart's home is for others.
It's in the chest—obviously!
But when it came to me
anatomy lost its mind.
Nothing but heart—
buzzing everywhere.
Oh, how many of them,
even the springs alone,
have been heaved into this imflamed body for 20 years!

Их груз нерастрáченный — прóсто неснóсен.
Неснóсен не так,
для стихá,
а буквáльно.

Their pent up burden is really unbearable.
Unbearable not
poetically,
but literally.

Что вы́шло

Бо́льше чем мо́жно,
бо́льше чем на́до —
бу́дто
поэ́товым бре́дом во сне нави́с —
комо́к серде́чный разро́сся грома́дой:
грома́да любо́вь,
грома́да не́нависть.
Под но́шей
но́ги
шага́ли ша́тко —
ты зна́ешь,
я же
ла́дно сла́жен —
и всё же
тащу́сь серде́чным прида́тком,
плеч подгиба́я косу́ю са́жень.
Взбуха́ю стихо́в молоко́м
— и не вы́литься —
не́куда, ка́жется — по́лнится за́ново.
Я вы́томлен ли́рикой —
ми́ра корми́лица,
гипе́рбола
прао́браза Мопасса́нова.

What came of it

Bigger than possible,
bigger than necessary—
as if
looming like a poet's delirious dream—
a lump of heart has expanded into a mass:
a mass of love;
a mass of hate.
Under this load
feet
step unsteadily—
you know,
I am
well-built,
and all the same
I drag myself along like the heart's appendix,
bending the broadness of my shoulders.
Engorged with the milk of poetry
—and I can't squeeze it out—
there's no place for it to flow, it seems—it just fills up again.
I'm utterly exhausted by lyrics—
the world's wet-nurse,
a hyperbole
of Maupassant's prototype.

Зову́

Подня́л силачо́м,
понёс акроба́том.
Как избира́телей сзыва́ют на ми́тинг,
как сёла
в пожа́р
созыва́ют наба́том —
я звал:
«А вот оно́!
Вот!
Возьми́те!»
Когда́
така́я махи́на а́хала —
не гля́дя,
пы́лью,
гря́зью,
сугро́бом,—
дамьё
от меня́
раке́той шара́халось:
«Нам что́бы поме́ньше,
нам вро́де танго́ бы...»
Нести́ не могу́ —
и несу́ мою но́шу.
Хочу́ её бро́сить —
и зна́ю,
не бро́шу!
Распо́ра не сде́ржат рёбровы ду́ги.
Грудна́я кле́тка треща́ла с нату́ги.

I’m calling

I lifted it like a strongman,
I carried it like an acrobat.
Like an alarm calling
voters to a meeting,
and villages
to a fire,
I yelled:
“Here it is!
Here!
Take it!”
When
an oaf like that goes crashing
without looking
through dust,
through dirt,
through a snowbank,
all the ladies
rush away like rockets:
“We need something smaller,
something more like a tango . . .”
I can’t carry it—
and I carry my load.
I want to throw it away—
and I know
I won’t!
The arches of my ribs won’t hold the thrusts.
My chest cracked from the strain.

Ты

Ты
пришла́ —
делови́то,
за ры́ком,
за ро́стом,
взгляну́в,
разгляде́ла про́сто ма́льчика.
Взяла́,
отобра́ла се́рдце
и про́сто
пошла́ игра́ть —
как де́вочка мя́чиком.
И ка́ждая —
чу́до бу́дто ви́дится —
где да́ма вкопа́лась,
а где деви́ца.
«Tako ́го люби́ть?
Да э́такий ри́нется!
Должно́, укроти́тельница.
Должно́, из звери́нца!»
А я лику́ю.
Нет его́ —
и́га!
От ра́дости себя́ не по́мня,
скака́л,
инде́йцем сва́дебным пры́гал,
так бы́ло ве́село,
бы́ло легко́ мне.

You

You
arrived—
businesslike,
behind my roar,
behind my height,
took one look,
and saw that I was a mere boy.
Without a second thought,
you took my heart away
and simply
went off to play—
like a girl with a ball.
And each of them
as if witnessing a miracle—
here a lady rooted herself to the ground—
over there, a damsel.
"Love someone like that?
That kind will lunge!
She must be an animal tamer.
Must be from the zoo!"
But I'm rejoicing.
It's gone—
that yoke!
Out of my mind with joy,
I was jumping,
I was leaping like an Indian wedding guest,
that's how happy I felt,
how light.

Невозмóжно

Одúн не смогý —
не снесý роя́ля
(тем бóлее —
несгорáемый шкаф).
А éсли не шкаф,
не рояль,
то я ли
сéрдце снёс бы, обрáтно взяв.
Банкúры знáют:
«Богáты без крáя мы.
Кармáнов не хвáтит —
кладём в несгорáемый».
Любóвь
в тебя́ —
богáтством в желéзо —
запря́тал,
хожý
и рáдуюсь Крéзом.
И рáзве,
éсли захóчется óчень,
улы́бку возьмý,
пол-улы́бки
и мéльче,
с другúми кутя́,
протрáчу в полнóчи
рублéй пятнáдцать лирúческой мéлочи.

Impossible

I can't do it alone—
I can't carry the grand piano
(much less—
the safe).
And if not a safe,
not a piano,
then how would I
carry my heart,
if I took it back?
Bankers know:
"We're rich beyond measure,
There aren't enough pockets—
let's put it in a safe."
I hid
my love
in you—
like riches in iron—
I walk around
and rejoice like Croesus.
And maybe,
if I really feel like it,
I'll withdraw a smile,
a half-smile,
even less,
and carousing with others,
in half a night I'll spend
about fifteen rubles worth of lyrical change.

Так и со мной

Флоты́ — и то стека́ются в га́вани.
По́езд — и то к вокза́лу го́нит.
Ну а меня́ к тебе́ и пода́вней —
я же люблю́! —
тя́нет и кло́нит.
Скупо́й спуска́ется пу́шкинский ры́царь
подва́лом свои́м любова́ться и ры́ться.
Так я
к тебе́ возвраща́юсь, люби́мая.
Моё это се́рдце,
любу́юсь мои́м я.
Домо́й возвраща́етесь ра́достно.
Грязь вы
с себя́ соскреба́ете, бре́ясь и мо́ясь.
Так я
к тебе́ возвраща́юсь, —
ра́зве,
к тебе́ идя́,
не иду́ домо́й я?!
Земны́х принима́ет земно́е ло́но.
К коне́чной мы возвраща́емся це́ли.
Так я
к тебе́
тяну́сь неукло́нно,
е́ле расста́лись,
разви́делись е́ле.

It's like that with me too

Even fleets—flow together into the harbor.
Even a train—pushes towards its station.
And all the even morer—
I love you!—
I'm dragged and inclined to you.
Pushkin's miserly knight goes down
to dig into and admire his cellar.
That's how I
return to you, my darling.
This is my heart
I revel in what's mine
You return home happily.
You scrape the dirt off yourself,
shaving and washing.
That's how I
return to you—
really
going to you,
am I not going home?!
The earth takes the earthly into its bosom.
We come back to our final end.
So I
reach inexorably
for you,
even though we've scarcely parted,
even though we've scarcely looked away from each other.

Вы́вод

Не смою́т любо́вь
ни ссо́ры,
ни вёрсты.
Проду́мана,
вы́верена,
прове́рена.
Подъе́мля торже́ственно стих строкопёрстый,
кляну́сь —
люблю́
неизме́нно и ве́рно!

1922

Conclusion

Neither quarrels
nor miles
will wash off love.
It's been thought over,
reconciled,
and verified.
Solemnly lifting a finger-lined verse
I swear—
I love you
irrevocably and faithfully.

Люблю/I love

In this cycle M assumes three distinct personas, two familiar, one new. In the first several poems, he's the poet/hooligan who rejects conventional society: while the human herd is drilled for labors, he runs around half-naked by the river; while young fools are schooled in "grammars," he bounces around the Moscow prison system; while college students learn geography from a miniature globe, he learns by sleeping on the ground; while fat cats talk to ladies, he talks to buildings; while businessmen are embraced by wives and lovers, he is embraced by the city streets.

But half-way through the cycle, with "Adult," "What happened," and "I call out," the tone moves from contempt to despair, and M assumes a second persona—the awkward goliath whose feelings are too intense and too enormous for the world. This is expressed with an extended metaphor, on which "I love" is constructed. The poet's heart, "a mass of love, a mass of hate," is a painful, ever increasing burden: in "Usually so," the sun wonders how there's room in the boy's heart for all it holds; in "Adult" the poet's heart is so stuffed with passions that it takes over his whole body; in "What happened" his body is a mere appendage to his heart, which he drags along, his shoulders straining; in "I call out," the weight finally becomes unbearable—the poet's ribs begin to crack and he is forced to yell out for help.

With "You," a third persona emerges—one that is not only new, but unique to "I Love"—the contented lover. The business-like Lilya responds to his cry, makes a quick assessment, and simply takes his heart as if it's a plaything. Relieved of his burden, he leaps for joy! His heart is now a wonderful treasure: he strolls around like Croesus, he can withdraw smiles whenever he likes, he admires his riches like Pushkin's miserly knight. In contrast to his pre-Lilya self—broke, lonely and homeless—he's rich, he's out carousing with friends, he has found his place in the world.

Обыкновенно так/How it usually is

The opening stanza describes the typical kind of love experienced by typical members of society: brief and inadequate.

очерствевает/to harden all over
The normal imperfective form is "черстветь." Adding the prefix "о" here probably indicates action directed over the whole area: to harden all over.

манжеты наделал/put on cuff
A pun on надел/наделал: put on/made a lot of.

Мужчина по Мюллеру мельницей машется/A man windmills according to Müller
M has made "махать" reflexive: probably meaning to windmill one's arms. The Müller exercise system (a 15 minute workout with no props) was very popular in the early years of the 20th century; even Franz Kafka was a devotee. M's friend David Burliuk was also a practitioner.

и груди стал заливать крахмалом/started to pour starch on breasts
"Груди" could be "breasts," but considering the context, it probably means shirt-fronts. It's not enough that the heart is enveloped in a body, and the body in clothes—now men also have to put on cuffs and starched shirtfronts as well.

скукожиться/to wither
A verb with comical overtones: to shrink or wither, like a deflating balloon. There also are less decent implications.

Мальчишкой/Boyhood

Mayakovsky spent his boyhood in a mountain village in the Caucasus, where his father worked as a forester. Most of the time he was outdoors, running around as described in this poem. From the chapter "Romantic Roots" in *I Myself*:

> "This was all on the territory of an ancient Georgian stronghold near Bagdadi. The fortress was enclosed by a rectangular rampart. Turrets at the corners for cannons. Gun-slots in the walls. Past the ramparts were moats. Past the moats, forests and jackals. Above the forests, mountains. I grew up. Ran to the top of the highest one. The mountains were lower to the north. To the north there was a gap. The Russia of my dreams was out there. I was unbelievably drawn to it."(1)

людьё/a herd of people
A collective form of "люди/people." Though M did not invent it, the word is extremely uncommon.

башмачного/shoed/with shoes on
Though not something you'll find in a typical Russian/English dictionary, "башмачный" is a normal word, not a Mayakovsky neologism.

играл с солдатьём под забором в «три листика»/I played "3 Leaves" by the fence with the soldiers"
Another collective noun: солдатьё, a gang of soldiers. "Под забором/under a fence" is the standard habitat of drunks, ruffians and bums. The card game Three Little Leaves is either Three-card Poker or Three-card Monte.

А тоже – с сердечком / Старается малым
Here "а тоже" means "and yet," or "despite the fact that." The sun is surprised: "I can barely see him / he's so tiny and yet he already has a heart." Heart is in the diminutive, and "малым" is its instrumental modifier: "He's doing the best he can with that little thing."

(1) Excerpts from *I Myself* are from James McGavran III, *Vladimir Mayakovsky: Selected Poems* (Northwestern University Press, 2013).

Юношей/As a youth

When M's father suddenly died in 1906, the family's "days of prosperity" were over. Left with "only 3 rubles" after the funeral, the family sold all their furniture and moved to Moscow. From *I Myself*:

> "Not enough to eat. A pension of 10 rubles a month. My sisters and I were in school. Mama had to rent out rooms and cook dinners. The rooms were crap."

M was far more interested in revolution than school, where he got "Ds and the occasional C for variety," and was soon getting arrested for distributing illegal literature, and for associating with organizers of robberies and prison breaks.

Грамматикам учим дурней и дур мы/We teach grammars to fools and foolets
As in English, "grammars" in the plural is unusual.

Лирики/Poets
This is the plural of "лирик/lyric poet."

кучерявые/curly-haired
A folksy variation of "курчавый/curly-haired."

в Бутырках/in Butyrka
At the age of 16, M was sent to Moscow's Butyrka prison for revolutionary activities, where he spent 5 months in solitary confinement.

Бюро похоронных процессий/the Funeral Home
Literally, the Bureau of Funeral Processions, the only building visible from his prison cell.

Чего, мол, стоют лучёнышки эти/What, they say, are these little rays worth
A very folksy conjugation of "стоить/to cost" (it should be "стоят").

за стенного за жёлтого зайца/a sunbeam along the wall
Literally, a yellow hare on the wall, meaning sun spots refracted through the window glass and moving across the walls and ceiling. The normal expression is "солнечный зайчик," a "sunny bunny," always in the diminutive, but M has "undiminutized" it.

Мой университет/My university

M's financial situation did not improve after his release from prison. David Burliuk kindly supplied him with 50 kopecks a day while the two were in art school, but M was still hungry and homeless. To keep from starving he had to rely on his winnings from card games and billiards.

Склоняете чудно/You decline marvelously
Like Latin and Greek, Russian has a grammatical system of declension. Nouns, pronouns, adjectives and numerals are declined according to case, gender, and number.

с домом спеться/to sing in harmony with the buildings
Literally, to "sing in harmony with," but the meaning is "to keep bad company."

наземь ночёвкой хлопаюсь!/I flop down on the ground for the night.
Not that he has nowhere to sleep but on the ground—rather, that he is so tired that he just falls asleep wherever he happens to be.

Мутят Иловайских больные вопросы/Painful questions torment the Ilovaiskis
Dmitry Ilovaiski was a writer of history textbooks.

Берут Добролюбова (чтоб зло ненавидеть),—фамилья ж против/They take Dobrolyubov (to learn to hate evil), the ancestral name itself is opposed
Nikolay Dobrolyubov was a socialist literary critic and journalist from the mid-19th century, whose name literally means "loving good." Naturally the name itself is opposed to evil.

мыслишки звякают лбёнками медненькими/their little thoughts jingle in brass foreheads
Both the noun and the adjective have diminutive suffixes here ("-ка" for "лбы", and "-енький" for "медные"). "Медный лоб/blockhead" is the type of blockhead who has a position of authority, like a policeman. It's not completely clear who has the brass foreheads though, is it the "fat and wealthy" men or the little thoughts themselves?

трещали, язык ворочая — флюгер/they wagged their weathervane tongues
Though "флюгер" is in the singular form here, the meaning is plural. Plural possessives modifying a singular noun is a standard grammatical construction in Russian.

Взрослое/An adult thing

“Взрослый” works as either a noun or an adjective. Here it has a neuter ending, meaning either he’s not a man, but some kind of creature, or that this is an “adult” poem (“стихотворение,” which is a neuter noun).

В рублях карманы
A mangled set phrase: instead of “money in my pockets,” it’s “pockets in money.”

Душой отдыхаете на жёнах, на вдовах/Soothe your soul with wives and widows
This looks like a combination of the expressions “глаза отдыхают на ком-то/чем-то/to find solace when looking at someone/something” and “отдохнуть душой/rest the soul.”

В сердца, в часишки любовницы тикают/Mistresses tick into hearts, into little watches
Considering the lines “Love? Of course! For a mere 100 rubles,” it seems that the “mistresses” who “tick in hearts and watches” are prostitutes: love is measured out in time and money, and the heart. And of course the heart itself ticks like a clock.

В восторге партнёры любовного ложа/Partners of love’s bed are in ecstasy
In the ’20s “партнёры” would not have been used to describe lovers—love’s bed has made them *business* partners.

Враспашку/unbuttoned
A distorted version of “нараспашку/unbuttoned.”

Что вышло/What came of it

What came of it? The transformation from delinquent to clown. His heart—"bigger than possible, bigger than necessary"—has made him vulnerable and ridiculous. This is the refrain from "To Himself," where the poet, "so big, so unnecessary," lumbers along, dragging his monstrous love behind him.

поэтовым/poets'

M. has tacked on the suffix "ов" (as in "Ivanov") to "poet" to create a novel form of the personal possessive.

плеч подгибая косую сажень/ bending the broadness of my shoulders

The normal expression is "косая сажень в плечах/a full *sazhen* in the shoulders" meaning broad-shouldered. (A *sazhen* is a measure of length, about 7 feet). M has rearranged the word order: "bending the full *sazhen* of my shoulders."

мира кормилица, гипербола праобраза Мопассанова/the world's wet-nurse, a hyperbole of Maupassant's archetype

This is a sharp contrast to the masculine image of wide shoulders, which you can imagine are bending from of the weight of his milk engorged breasts! "A hyperbole of Maupassant" refers to the short story "The Idyll," which describes a mutually beneficial encounter between a wet-nurse and a starving young peasant. Maupassant's stories were racy by Russian standards and widely popular. M's contemporary Isaac Babel also featured "The Idyll" in his story "Guy de Maupassant," where a young "starving artist" accepts a proposition from a wealthy (and busty) benefactress.

Зову/I'm calling

In earlier poems M's anguished cries to his beloved/the universe are met with indifference (e.g. his repeated screams of "Maria! Maria! Maria!" in "A cloud in trousers," or his cries to God in "A few words about myself" or "Backbone-flute"). This may be the only example where his pleas for help ("Here it is! Here! Take it!") are actually answered.

такая махина ахала/an oaf like me would crash
"Ахать" is an expression of surprise or horror, but does not necessarily have to be verbal. In this case, it seems he's lumbering around, out of control, alarmed by his own movements.

дамьё/a herd of ladies
Another exceedingly rare collective noun.

Ты/You

The arrival of Lilya marks the climax of the cycle, and maybe also of M's life. It seems like his happiest years were from that "most joyous date" in July, 1915, when he "made the acquaintance of L.Y. and O.M. Brik" through the early '20s, when he directed his creative powers to the fervent support of the new Soviet republic. He had found love, a home and a purpose.

за рыком, за ростом/behind my roar, behind my height
As if his "height" and his "roar" are just a façade.

Взяла/Took
A small pun, as there are 2 meanings: "to take," but also "to do something suddenly and unexpectedly."

отобрала/took
To take something that doesn't belong to you.

где дама вкопалась, а где девица/here a lady dug in, there a damsel
"Дама" and "девица" would be members of Russian high society from the days of Tolstoy, maybe a countess, and a young lady making her debut at a ball.

Должнó/most likely
Short for "должнó быть." If the accent was on the first syllable ("дóлжно"), the meaning would change. "It's necessary to . . . "

зверинца/zoo
More precisely, "menagerie," a collection of exotic animals, which you could find on the royal grounds of a 17th century monarch. It can also mean "an odd assortment of characters."

ига/burden
It's clear that the yoke is his heart: the words "иго/yoke" and "сердце/heart" share the same gender (neuter).

индейцем свадебным/Indian wedding guest
Mayakovsky may have been inspired by the wedding scene in Longfellow's "Hiawatha," where Pau-Puk-Keewis performs "his mystic dance." "Hiawatha" was translated by Ivan Bunin in 1896, and was widely read in Russia.

Невозможно/Impossible

Safe in Lilya's possession, his heart is an inexhaustible source of riches, from which he can make withdrawals of happiness.

И разве/And really

This can either be an expression of disbelief, as in "разве ты не знаешь," or a possibility to entertain, as in "what if I . . . ?"

протрачу/burn through

With the prefix "про", M has amplified the meaning of "тратить/to spend."

Так и со мной/It’s like that with me too

Just as ships have their harbors, as a train has its station, as foxes have dens and birds have nests, the poet too finally has a home. It’s like that with him too, but even more so!

подавней/all the more

M has, very amusingly, made the adverb “подавно/all the more” a comparative: “all the morer.”

Вывод/Conclusion

Unlike the mere mortals in the opening poem "Usually so," who have to squeeze in a little love between "jobs, profits and so forth," and for whom love "blooms for a moment . . . and withers," M has found a love suitable for the gods—one that can't be washed away; that has been verified and reconciled; that is solemn, grand and eternal.

строкопёрстый/finger-lined

The immediate association is the epithet "розоперстая Аврора/rosy-fingered dawn" from *The Odyssey*. There are other associations: the Greek word for "finger" is "dactyl;" a dactyl is a three-syllable poetic unit; dactylic meter is the meter of classic epic poetry—the meter of Homer. Like Odysseus returning home to Penelope, the hero of this epic saga—undaunted by battles and distance—vows to love resolutely and eternally.

О дря́ни

Сла́ва, Сла́ва, Сла́ва геро́ям!!!
Впро́чем,
им
дово́льно возда́ли да́ни.
Тепе́рь
поговори́м
о дря́ни.

Утихоми́рились бу́ри революцио́нных лон.
Подёрнулась ти́ной сове́тская мешани́на.
И вы́лезло
из-за спины́ РСФСР
мурло́
мещани́на.

(Меня́ не пойма́ете на сло́ве,
я во́все не про́тив меща́нского сосло́вия.
Меща́нам
без разли́чия кла́ссов и сосло́вий
моё славосло́вие.)

Со всех необъя́тных росси́йских нив,
с пе́рвого дня сове́тского рожде́ния
стекли́сь они́,
на́скоро опере́нья переменя́в,
и засе́ли во все учрежде́ния.

Намозо́лив от пятиле́тнего сиде́ния зады́,
кре́пкие, как умыва́льники,
живу́т и поны́не
ти́ше воды́.
Сви́ли ую́тные кабине́ты и спа́ленки.

И ве́чером
та и́ли ина́я мразь,
на жену́.
за пиани́ном обуча́ющуюся, гля́дя,
говори́т,
от самова́ра разморя́сь:

About trash

Glory, Glory, Glory to the heroes!
But
they've
received enough tribute.
Now
let's talk
about trash.

The storms of the revolutionary wombs have quieted.
The Soviet jumble is covered with slime.
And the ugly face
of the *meshchanin*
has crawled out
from behind the back of the Socialist Republic.

(Don't misunderstand me,
I'm not against the middle class itself.
My words of glory
are for philistines,
not discriminating against any class.)

They thronged in
from all the vast Russian fields,
from the first day of the Soviet birth,
and quickly changing their feathers,
inhabited all establishments.

Their behinds calloused from five years of sitting,
hardened like wash-basins,
they live to this very day
quieter than water.
They've woven comfortable offices and little bedrooms.

And in the evening
this or that scum,
overheated from drinking too much tea,
looking over at his wife,
who's practicing at the piano,
says

«Товáрищ Нáдя!
К празднику прибáвка -
24 тыщи.
Тарúф.
Эх, заведý я себé
тихоокеáнские галифúща,
чтоб из штанóв
выглядывать
как корáлловый риф!»
А Нáдя:
«И мне с эмблéмами плáтья.
Без серпá и мóлота не покáжешься в свéте!
В чём
сегóдня
бýду фигурять я
на балý в Рéввоéнсовéте?!»
На стéнке Маркс.
Рáмочка áла.
На «Извéстиях» лёжа, котёнок грéется.
А из-под потолóчка
верещáла
оголтéлая канарéица.

Маркс со стéнки смотрéл, смотрéл...
И вдруг
разúнул рот,
да как заорёт:
«Опýтали революцию обывáтельщины нúти.
Страшнée Врáнгеля обывáтельский быт.
Скорée
гóловы канарéйкам свернúте -
чтоб коммунúзм
канарéйками не был побúт!»

1921

"Comrade Nadia!
For the holiday I got an additional
24 thousand
added to my pay.
I'll get myself
some oceanic riding-breeches,
so my pants will stick out
and look as amazing
as a coral reef!"
And Nadia:
"And I'll get dresses with emblems.
You can't go out in society without showing your hammer and sickle!
What
am I going to show off in
today
at the Revolutionary War Council ball?!"
On the wall there's a Marx
in a little red frame.
A kitten is curled up on *The News*.
A frenzied canary
chirped
beneath the little ceiling.

From the wall Marx looked, and looked . . .
And suddenly,
his mouth gaping,
he roars out:
"Bourgeois threads have tangled the revolution.
Bourgeois life is more terrible than Wrangle.
Better
to twist off the canaries' heads
so communism
is not beaten down by canaries!"

О драни/About trash

From Mayakovsky's last public speech:

> "I have worked my whole life, but not to make pretty little things, and to caress men's ears. And somehow matters have always turned out in such a way as to create unpleasantness for everybody. My basic work is to curse and ridicule whatever seems wrong to me and what we need to fight against. For the most part, the twenty years of my literary work have been, to put it plainly, a literary face punching. Not literally, but in the best sense! Every minute it's been necessary to defend this or that revolutionary position in literature . . . and to fight against that stagnation which we are still encountering in our 13-year old republic." (1)

The face that gets punched here belongs to the petty Soviet official, a figure that M mercilessly satirized through the '20s. In the poem "Прозаседавшиеся/All meetinged out," civil servants split themselves in half so as to attend as many meetings as possible, ignoring the needs of an ordinary citizen stranded in the waiting room. In *The Bedbug*, the former worker Prisypkin uses his proletarian credentials to acquire all kinds of bourgeois "trash"—fancy knickknacks from the private market, a trophy wife, and even an aristocratic sounding new name—"Pierre Violin." In *The Bathhouse* the bureau chief Pobedonosikov makes pompous speeches, has his portrait painted and plans elaborate vacations for himself, while fending off the supplicants lined up outside his door. These characters pay lip service to the ideals of communism while indulging in all the vulgarity, vanity and callousness of the bourgeois class that had supposedly been eradicated.

Слава, Слава, Слава/Glory, Glory, Glory

When first published in the periodical *Bov*, the poem appeared after a eulogy to fallen heroes of the Russian Civil War, the last line of which was "Glory! Glory! Glory!"(2) An elegant transition from that armed conflict to the new cultural war on the domestic front.

Утихомирились бури революционных лон/Storms of revolutionary wombs

The biblical word "лоно/womb," is peculiar here since it's in the plural. It's generally only used in the singular in set phrases, e.g. "на лоне природы/in the bosom of nature."

---

(1) I. Slavinsky, "Poslednee vystuplenie Vladimira Vladimirovicha Mayakovskogo " *V. Maiakovskii v vospominaniiakh sovremenikov*. (Moscow, 1963).

(2) Brown, 222.

я вовсе не против меща́нского сословия/I'm not against the middle class
In other words, "I'm not against the lower-middle class itself (which existed before the revolution), but against the 'low-class person' as he appears in any level of society. " A *meshchanin* is a coarse person with aspirations for higher status and comforts, unconcerned with the needs of anyone but himself.

и засели во все учреждения/sat themselves down in all establishments
They "засели/sat themselves down" and "заседали/had a meeting," thus the calloused bottoms.

Свили уютные кабинеты и спаленки/The wove comfy offices and little bedrooms
There are many references to birds: the Soviet philistines throng in from the fields, they change their feathers, weave little rooms, and keep pet canaries.

за пианином/at the piano
"Пианино/piano" is an indeclinable noun, but here it appears with an instrumental ending. This pretentious official is poorly educated. Zoschenko's short stories from the '20s are full of this kind of mangled language, characteristic of the lower classes of workers and peasants as they attempted to integrate themselves into post-revolutionary society.

от самовара разморясь/getting overheated from the samovar
Not just overheated but also sated and drowsy: "melting down."

тихоокеанские галифища/pacific oceanic galifé
"Galifé" were riding style breeches worn (originally) by high ranking officers in the cavalry. The suffix "ще" makes these pants even wider—like the Pacific Ocean.

чтоб из штанов выглядывать как коралловый риф!»
Literally: "so that I'll stick out of my pants to look like a coral reef!"

Реввоенсовет/Rev-Mil-Soviet
An acronym for the "Revolutionary War Council." This ultra Soviet establishment is throwing a ball, something that should have been abolished with the revolution—the bourgeoisie has been newly incarnated in the bosom of communist society.

На стенке Маркс/There's a Marx
As part of the campaign to eradicate religion, the traditional Russian Orthodox icon corner was replaced with the "red corner," which featured portraits of communist

heroes, news articles, and inspirational slogans. Every school, public institution, and ideologically correct household had "a Marx" displayed in this place of honor.

На "Известиях" лёжа, котёнок греется/A kitten warms itself, lying on *Izvestia*
A major Soviet newspaper serves as a floor cover for their kitty.

А из-под потолочка/from underneath a little ceiling
As if the apartment itself is a cozy little nest.

Страшнее Врангеля обывательский быт/The Philistine lifestyle is more terrible than Wrangel
Baron Pyotr Wrangel was the commanding general of the White Army during the Russian Civil War. The Civil War is over, but the battle for communism continues in private homes.

Скорее головы канарейкам сверните/It's better to wring the canaries' necks
An innocent canary becomes the symbol of petty bourgeois life—of *byt*.

The Bolshevik aesthetic tilted heavily towards the austere. After all, for the committed revolutionary a comfortable home life was out of the question. Indulging one's petty desires was frowned upon—the revolution required complete devotion, even at the cost of health, family and life itself. Personal effects were ideally limited to what could be carried—one had to be responsive to the call of duty. Lenin himself had a famously Spartan lifestyle, and even after his life on the run culminated in Bolshevik victory, he furnished his Kremlin apartment with only the bare necessities.

With the establishment of communism, the Bolsheviks imagined that a New Soviet Man would emerge to carry on this tradition of self-sacrifice. This ideal citizen, disregarding personal preferences and comforts, and inspired by their love for the communal, would work relentlessly to ensure the happiness of future generations. In the upcoming utopian society, there would be no private property, private space, private time and even, perhaps, no private identity.

After Lenin's War Communism policies had destroyed the Russian economy and provoked a backlash that nearly unseated him from power, the Bolsheviks were forced to retreat from their ideological position and allow the return of a degree of private enterprise. When the New Economic Policy started to take effect, ideologues were distressed to see that not only that private citizens, but also party members were succumbing to the old bourgeois norms of cozy domesticity (the hissing samovar, the wife practicing at the piano, house pets, kitschy artwork) and the quest for status items (the galifé, the emblems). The duties of enforcing the communist ideal were thus transferred from the Red Army to the artistic community. Mayakovsky and *LEF* were at the vanguard of this cultural war, with the mission of depicting the new Soviet *byt*.

It turned out that attacking old style *byt* was a lot easier than providing alternatives. The items created by the Constructivists for the New Soviet Man—convertible furniture, multi-purpose unisex clothing, architecture for communal buildings—never took hold. It could be argued that M himself failed miserably in modeling the new Soviet consciousness: though his tiny apartment on Lubyanka Passage in Moscow, like Lenin's, contained only what was necessary for work and existence, he was certainly guilty of indulging his own bourgeois tastes. He dutifully fulfilled Lilya's requests to purchase all kinds of luxury items on his trips abroad. One such shopping list included stockings, a pearl necklace, Rue de la Paix perfume, Brun eyebrow pencils, a dress of "crêpe georgette with petticoat' *and* a car (a Renault, including car gloves).[(3)] Perhaps it's not astounding that after writing so passionately about wringing canary necks, he actually gifted his beloved with a pet song bird in a cage.

(3) Jangfeldt, 411.

Проща́нье

В авто́,
последний франк разменя́в.
- В кото́ром часу́ на Марсе́ль? -
Пари́ж
бежи́т,
провожа́я меня́,
во всей
невозмо́жной красе́.
Подступа́й
к глаза́м,
разлу́ки жи́жа,
се́рдце
мне
сентимента́льностью расква́сь!
Я хоте́л бы
жить
и умере́ть в Пари́же,
Е́сли б не́ было
такой земли́ -
Москва́.

1925

Farewell

In an automobile,
exchanging my last franc.
“What time is the train to Marseilles?”
Paris
is running,
seeing me off,
in all
its impossible beauty.
Rise up
to my eyes,
slush of parting,
Melt down
my heart
with sentimentality!
I’d want to
live
and die in Paris,
If there was no
such land
as M o s c o w.

Прощанье/Farewell

Of all the European cities, Paris made the greatest impression on M, and even inspired a whole collection of poems. "Farewell" is the last of the "Paris" cycle, written during his second visit to the city in the fall of 1924.

Russians have viewed Paris through a sentimental haze since the days of Catherine the Great, and it's not strange that M too was captivated by its beauty. But there were also personal ties. In the '20s Paris was a major center of Russian emigration, the new home to many of the best of Russia's avant-garde (Sergei Diaghilev, Igor Stravinsky, Marc Chagall, Marina Tsvetaeva, and M's old friends Goncharova and Larionov, to name a few). M was naturally drawn to the Paris art scene—Russian Futurism, after all, had been tremendously impacted by Cubism, and in his circle of friends from the teens, Picasso was idolized. When M visited Paris for the first time in 1922, Diaghilev took him for a tour of studios and galleries, and introduced him not only to the great Picasso himself, but to the lesser gods Braque, Fernand Léger, Robert Delaunay, and Jean Cocteau. The result was the short book *A Seven-day Overview of French Painting*, in which M, while acknowledging the achievements of the Parisians, concludes that contemporary Russian art is superior—after all, in the communist land of "M o s c o w," everything is naturally superior.(1)

M's own art training is evident in this poem, which is laid out in his trademark "*lesenka*" or "staircase" style. *Lesenka* is an evolution of the column format: cutting the lines up this way allowed M to further transcend the limits of punctuation, using space to indicate pauses, emphases and intonation. But *lesenka* is not only a means of sculpting sound—it also has a strong visual impact. M developed the format in 1923, the same year he was creating his marvelous ads with Rodchenko, with their masterful and inventive layout of text and image.(2) It's possible that *lesenka* grew out of these experiments in graphic design.

M stuck with the format for the rest of his career, using it even in his suicide note and final signature:

---

(1) M even invited Picasso to relocate from Paris to Moscow, where, instead of canvases, he could paint entire buildings for May Day celebrations. "With us," he said, "there is freedom without limit." Bykov, 543.

(2) M considered his adwork, produced on behalf of state entities such as the food cooperative "Mossleprom," the department store "GUM," the Rubber Trust, the Pencil Trust, and the "Tea Establishment," to be "to be poetry of the highest qualification." The ads fulfilled of the Constructivist idea of "production art"—that art should serve the needs of the people, and was no less valid than so-called "pure art." This view was validated several months after this poem was written, when at the International Exhibition of Modern Decorative and Industrial Arts in Paris, M's advertising posters won a silver medal.

Как говорят:	As they say:
«инцидент исперчен»	"the case is closed"
Любовная лодка	Love's boat
разбилась о быт	has crashed on mundanity
Я с жизнью в расчёте	Life and I are quits
и не к чему перечень	and there's no use in listing
взаимных болей,	our mutual hurts
бед	sorrows
и обид	and resentments
Счастливо оставаться	Stay happy
Владимир	Vladimir
Маяковский	Mayakovsky

сантиментальностью/with sentimentality

Instead of the standard "сентиментальность," M uses an old fashioned spelling, with an "a." "Прощанье" also has an old style spelling, ending in "ье" rather than "ие"—something you'd see in a Pushkin poem. This supports the tender, nostalgic tone of the poem.

расквась/turn to mush

The imperative of "расквасить," which literally means "to turn into kvass." It's used in two contexts, both referring to the face. The idea is that the features of the face become indistinct, either from a bruising or bloody nose from a scuffle ("beat to a pulp" would be too strong), or because the face contains so many fluids that they can't be contained – as with a bad head cold.

жижа—Париже; расквась—Москва/slush—Paris; mush—Moscow

Both cities get very funny rhymes, which undercuts any sentimentality.

такой земли—М о с к в а/such a land as M o s c o w

Moscow is not just a city, not just the capital of the Russian Soviet Republic, but a magical "land" holding all the promise of communism. M's position on Moscow vs the West is nicely summed up in this short account from Marina Tsvetaeva:

> On 22 April 1922, the eve of my departure from Russia, early in the morning, on the completely deserted Kuznetsky I met Mayakovsky.
> "Well then, Mayakovsky, what message do you want me to pass on to Europe?"
> "That the truth is over here." (3)

(3) From a "salutation" to Mayakovsky, published in D.S. Mirsky's journal "Eurasia," 1928.

Бродве́й

Асфа́льт - стекло́.
Иду́ и звеню́.
Леса́ и трави́нки
— сбри́ты.
На се́вер
с ю́га
иду́т авеню́,
на за́пад с восто́ка
— стри́ты.
А ме́жду —
(куда́ их строи́тель завёз!) —
дома́
невозмо́жной длины́.
Одни́
дома́ длино́й до звёзд,
други́е
— длино́й до луны́.
Я́нки
подо́швами шлёпать
лени́в:
просто́й
и курье́рский лифт.
В 7 часо́в
челове́чий прили́в,
В 17 часо́в -
отли́в.
Скреже́щет меха́ника,
звон и гам,
а лю́ди
немы́е в зво́не.
И лишь замелдя́ют
жева́ть чуинга́м,
чтоб бро́сить:
«Мек мо́ней?»
Мама́ша
грудь
ребёнку дала́.

Broadway

The asphalt is glass.
I walk and jingle.
The forests and blades of grass —
shaven off.
Avenues go
from south
to north,
streets
—from east to west.
And in-between—
(right where their builder dropped them!)
are buildings
of impossible height.
Some
buildings go up to the stars,
others
up to the moon.
Yankees
are reluctant
to slap their soles:
thus you have the regular
and the express elevator.
At 7 o'clock
there's a human tide,
At 5 o'clock—
an ebb.
Mechanisms grind,
a ringing and uproar,
but people
are mute in the ringing.
And only slow down
their gum chewing
to snap:
"Make money?"
Mumsy
gave
her breast to a child.

Ребёнок
с ка́плями и́з но́су,
сосёт
как бу́дто
не грудь, а долла́р —
за́нят
серьёзным
би́знесом.
Рабо́та око́нчена.
Те́ло обве́й
в сплошно́й
электри́ческий ве́тер.
Хо́чешь под зе́млю
— бери́ собве́й,
на не́бо
— бери́ элеве́йтер.
Ваго́ны
е́дут
и ды́мам под рост,
и в пя́тках
домо́вьих
тру́тся,
и вы́несут
хвост
на Бру́клинский мост,
и спря́чут
в но́ры
под Гу́дзон.
Тебя́ ослепи́ло,
ты
осове́л.
Но,
как бараба́нная дробь,
из тьмы
по те́мени:
«Ко́фе Максве́л
гуд
ту ди ласт дроп».
А ла́мпы
как ста́нут
ночь копа́ть,

The child
with his nose running,
sucks
as if
it's not a breast, but a dollar—
he's engaged
in serious
business.
Work is finished.
Fan the body
in the perfectly
electric wind.
If you want to go underground—
take the subway,
or to the sky—
take the elevated train.
The subway cars
go
almost up to the smoke
and rub themselves
in the heels
of buildings,
and display
their tails
on the Brooklyn bridge,
and hide
in burrows
under the Hudson.
You're blinded,
you're
in a stupor.
But,
like a drum roll,
on the top of your head
out from the darkness there's:
"Coffee Maksvel
gud
to dee last drop."
And lights
begin
digging in the night,

ну, я доложу́ вам

– пла́мечко!

Нале́во посмо́тришь

— ма́мочка мать!

Напра́во

— мать моя́ ма́мочка!

Есть что погляде́ть моско́вской братве́.

И за́ день

в коне́ц не дойду́т.

Это Нью-Йо́рк.

Это Бродве́й.

Гау ду ю ду!

Я в восто́рге

от Нью-Йо́рка го́рода.

Но

кепчо́нку

не сдёрну с виска́.

У сове́тских

со́бственная го́рдость:

на буржу́ев

смо́трим свысока́.

1926

well, I'll tell you—
                    that's some flame!
Take a look on the left—
                        holy moly!
on the right—
                moly's holy moly!
Here's something for the Moscow gang to see.
Even in a day
                you won't reach the end.
This is New York.
                    This is Broadway.
Gow do you do!
I'm euphoric
                over New York City.
But
    I won't
            doff my cap.
The Soviets
            have their pride:
we look down
                on the bourgeoisie.

Бродвей/Broadway

It's hard to imagine a more poem-worthy subject. At the height of the Roaring Twenties, the premier agitator for the communist revolution visits New York City—the very heart of capitalism—and takes a stroll along Broadway. You might expect a harsh critique, but no, he's overwhelmed and delighted by the technology: buildings reaching to the stars, local and express elevators, subways flashing their tails, the electric signage at night. It's not until the end of the poem that he suddenly remembers that he's a good Soviet citizen among the "bourgies." And though he doesn't explain why he won't "doff his cap," we can guess at the source of his "Soviet pride."

The US might be a "technological fantasy land," as M wrote in his travel log *My Discovery of America*, but its ideological basis is rotten. "There isn't a country that spits out as much moralistic, lofty, idealistic, sanctimonious rubbish as the United States." Behind the rhetoric, the truth is clear: America's real religion is money. "God is the dollar. The dollar is the Father. The dollar is the holy ghost." Any type of behavior is justifiable if there is money to be made, and no one blinks at the callous exploitation of factory workers, the unjust treatment of Negroes, the degradation of women or the brutal slaughtering of animals. The furious construction of buildings, roads and factories, the torrents of electricity, the massive transport of the population via train, subway, car, and gridded streets with traffic lights, the assembly lines, the automated slaughter houses—all of this is not for the benefit of the people, but for the benefit of the Capitalists. The Soviets, on the other hand, are not driven by the desire to "mek money," but to harness technology "in humanity's interests." (1)

M consistently does his part to perpetuate the Russian national myth—the idea that in some indefinable, elusive, abstract way, the country of Russia and its people are superior to all others. Russia may appear to be simple and backward, but since the days of Ivan the Terrible, the country has imagined itself as the key holder to some brand of world utopia. Whether it was the czars' claims to be the protectors and upholders of true Christianity,(2) Dostoevsky's belief that Russia was the cradle of a new universal literature,(3) or the Soviet insistence that authentic communism emanated only from Moscow, the template is the same: the savior of the world is Russia.

---

(1) Excepts are from Vladimir Mayakovsky, *My Discovery of America,* trans by Neil Cornwell (Hesperus Press Limited, 2006).

(2) After the fall of Constantinople, Moscow became the new center of Eastern Orthodox Christianity, and Russians sometimes imagined their capital as a "Third Rome."

(3) In his "Pushkin speeh" from 1880, Dostoevsky presented the idea that "pan-humanism," as expressed in the writing of Pushkin, was a characteristic of the Russian soul, and that Russia had the capacity (and duty!) to bring all of humanity together in a brotherly union "in accordance with the gospel of Christ."

куда их строитель завёз/where their builder left them

This is an expression of surprise—not "This is where they were brought," but "Wow, look where they are!"

невозможной длины/of an impossible height

M uses the colloquial "длина/length" instead of "высота/height."

бери элевейтер/take the elevated train.

Elevated trains were a NYC feature from the 1880's through the 1950's.

Мамаша/Mama

A fairly derogatory term for a matronly, middle-class woman. This is a strong colloquial *Russian* word, and it's jarring to apply it to a New Yorker. In this poem M alternates between phonetic renditions of American words ("avenue," "streets," "Yankee," "chewing gum," "make money," etc.) and Russian colloquialisms ("невозможной длины/of impossible length" "братве/the gang" "буржуев/bourgies"). This has a madcap effect, as if M has assumed the persona of a country bumpkin or Ivan the Fool, and overwhelmed by the marvels of a foreign city, is reeling between vocabularies.

дымам под рост/smoke

Smoke in the plural, suggesting different colors or shades of smoke from multiple sources.

Тело обвей в сплошной электрический ветер/Fan your body in the completely electric wind

"обвеять/to fan" is not a common verb, and is always accompanied by the noun "веер/fan" in the instrumental case. Here it's an imperative, which itself is almost unthinkable, and the accompanying noun is not in the instrumental, but the accusative. This is suggestive of something much more tangible, like wrapping yourself up in a shawl.

в пятках домовьих трутся/rub themselves in the buildings' heels

A very aggressive personification, since possessive adjectives are reserved for living beings (e.g. коровий/belonging to a cow; бабий/belonging to grandmother, человечий/belonging to humans), never for inanimate objects.

The verb "тереться" is suggestive of a cat rubbing up against its owner's legs ("кошки трутся о ноги").

Кофе Максве́л/Coffee Maksvel

The brand name and slogan for Maxwell House Coffee is rendered phonetically in Russian. The stress on the second syllable of "Maksvel," is for the sake of the rhyme (осове́л/Максве́л).

под Гу́дзон/under the Hudson

The normal stress in Russian would be Гудзо́н, but M wants it to rhyme with тру́тся.

А лампы/and streetlights

Probably not just streetlights, but all the lights.

пламечко/a little conflagration

Another impossible word, since "пламя/flame" is never in the diminutive.

на буржуев смотрим свысока/We look down on the bourgeoisie

The derogatory term "буржуй" is a colloquialism of "буржуа/member of the bourgeoisie." This word made its poetic debut in the couplet:

> Ешь ананасы, рябчиков жуй,
> День твой последний приходит, буржуй.
>
> Eat your pineapples, chew on your game hen,
> Your last day is coming, bourgeois vermin.

These lines came to M one evening in the fall of 1917, as he was observing the "remnants of fashionable and rich Petersburg" crowding around the entrance of one of the bohemian cafes he frequented, and the couplet was published soon afterwards in the short-lived Bolshevik newspaper "The Nightingale." M was especially proud of this little poem. He quoted it in his epic "Vladimir Ilych Lenin," and bragged about the fact that the Kronstadt sailors, as they stormed the Winter Palace at the climax of the October Revolution, were chanting the words "eat your pineapples, chew on your grouse . . ."

The term «буржуй» also famously appears in Alexander Blok's 1918 poem "The Twelve":

> Мы на горе всем буржуям
> Мировой пожар раздуем!
> Мировой пожар в крови—
> Господи, благослови!

To the sorrow of all the bourgies
We'll fan a worldwide conflagration!
A conflagration drenched in blood —
Give us your blessing, oh Lord!

Домо́й!

Уходи́те, мы́сли, во-своя́си.
Обними́сь,
души́ и мо́ря глубь.
Тот,
кто постоя́нно я́сен —
тот,
по-мо́ему,
про́сто глуп.
Я в ху́дшей каю́те
из всех каю́т —
всю ночь на́до мно́ю
нога́ми кую́т.
Всю ночь,
поко́й потолка́ возмути́в,
несётся та́нец,
сто́нет моти́в:
«Марки́та,
Марки́та,
Марки́та моя́,
заче́м ты,
Марки́та,
не лю́бишь меня́…»
А заче́м
люби́ть меня́ Марки́те?!
У меня́
и фра́нков да́же нет.
А Марки́ту
(то́лечко моргни́те!)
за́ сто фра́нков
препрово́дят в кабине́т.
Небольши́е де́ньги —
поживи́ для ши́ку —
нет,
интеллиге́нт,
взбива́я грязь вихро́в,
бу́дешь всу́чивать ей
шве́йную маши́нку,
по стёжкам
строча́щую

Homeward!

Off you go, thoughts, back home.
Embrace,
            depths of soul and sea.
Someone
            who's always in good spirits
is someone who,
                        in my opinion,
                                        is simply stupid.
Of all the cabins,
I'm in the worst cabin of all—
feet are hammering
                        above me all night long.
All night,
            disturbing the ceiling's peace,
the sounds of dancing,
                            a tune is groaning:
"Marquita,
              Marquita,
Marquita my dear,
                        why
                            don't you love me
Marquita my dear..."
And why
            would Marquita love me?!
I don't have
                a single franc.
But for a hundred,
they'll send Marquita
to your cabin
(you only have to wink!)
If there's not much money,
                                spend it in style—
but no,
Mr. Intellectual.
You'll fluff up your dirty forelocks,
and force
            a sewing machine on her,
that scribbles
                the silk of your poetry

шелка́ стихо́в.
Пролета́рии
прихо́дят к коммуни́зму
ни́зом —
ни́зом шахт,
серпо́в
и вил, —
я ж
с небе́с поэ́зии
броса́юсь в коммуни́зм,
потому́ что
нет мне
без него́ любви́.
Всё равно́ —
сосла́лся сам я
или по́слан к ма́ме —
слов ржаве́ет сталь,
черне́ет ба́са медь.
Почему́
под иностра́нными дождя́ми
вымока́ть мне,
гнить мне
и ржаве́ть?
Вот лежу́,
уе́хавший за во́ды,
ле́нью
е́ле дви́гаю
мое́й маши́ны ча́сти.
Я себя́
сове́тским чу́вствую
заво́дом,
выраба́тывающим сча́стье.
Не хочу́,
чтоб меня́, как цвето́чек с поля́н,
рва́ли
по́сле служе́бных тя́гот.
Я хочу́,
чтоб в деба́тах
поте́л Госпла́н,
мне дава́я
зада́ния на́ год.

in stiches.

Proletariats
come to communism
from the bottom—
from the low road of mines,
sickles,
and pitchforks—
As for me,
I throw myself into communism
from the heavens of poetry,
because
without it,
love doesn't exist for me.
It's all the same
whether I leave willingly
or I'm sent packing—
The steel of words gets rusty,
the brass of my bass gets tarnished.
Why is it my lot
to get soaked
and rot
and rust
under foreign rain?
Here I lie,
having set off over the sea,
barley moving
the pieces of my machinery
out of laziness.
I feel
like a Soviet
factory,
manufacturing happiness.
I don't want
to be plucked
like a blossom from the fields
after a hard day at work.
I want
the State Planning Committee
to sweat in debates,
giving me
my assignment for the year.

Я хочу́,

чтоб над мы́слью

времён комисса́р

с приказа́нием нависа́л.

Я хочу́,

чтоб сверхста́вками спе́ца

получа́ло

любо́вищу се́рдце.

Я хочу́

чтоб в конце́ рабо́ты

завко́м

запира́л мои́ гу́бы

замко́м.

Я хочу́,

чтоб к штыку́

приравня́ли перо́.

С чугуно́м чтоб

и с вы́делкой ста́ли

о рабо́те стихо́в,

от Политбюро́,

что́бы де́лал

докла́ды Ста́лин.

«Так, мол,

и так…

И до са́мых верхо́в

прошли́

из ра́бочих нор мы:

в Сою́зе

Респу́блик

понима́нье стихо́в

вы́ше

довое́нной но́рмы…»

Я хочу́ быть по́нят мое́й страно́й,

а не бу́ду по́нят—

что ж.

По родно́й стране́

пройду́ стороно́й,

как прохо́дит

косо́й дождь.

1925

I want
Commissar Time
to loom over me
with an order.
I want
for my heart to receive
a gigantic love
at the highest rate paid to specialists.
I want
the factory committee
to lock my lips
shut
at the end of the work day.
I want
my pen to be regarded
as a bayonet.
For Stalin
to deliver reports
from the Politburo
on the processing of poetry
along with the production
of iron and steel.
"Here's how
it is . . .
from the working class burrows
we have made it
to the very heights:
in the Soviet
Republics
the understanding of poetry
has exceeded
the pre-war norm.
I want to be understood by my country,
And if I'm not understood—
then what can I do.
I'll pass over
my native land
without notice,
like slanted rain.

Домой!/Homeward!

"Homeward" contains several passages of sustained regular meter, unusual for Mayakovsky. The opening lines (excepting the last 3 syllables) are trochaic, as if arising from the choppy sea:

Уходи́те, мы́сли, во-своя́си.
Обними́сь, души́ и мо́ря глубь.
Тот, кто постоя́нно я́сен —
тот, по-мо́ему, про́сто глуп.

/ u / u / u / u /
Off you go, my thoughts, away, back home.
/ u / u / u / u /
Let the depths of sea and soul embrace
/ u / u / u /
He who's cheerful without fail
/ u / u / u /
Must be someone who's a dope.

The "groaning tune" about Marquita is amphibrachic:

Марки́та, Марки́та, Марки́та моя,
заче́м ты, Марки́та, не лю́бишь меня́…

u /u u /u u /u u /
Marquita, Marquita, Marquita, my dear,
u / u u / u u / u u /
I know you don't love me, but why is unclear. . .

And the wish list that concludes the poem consists of 6 nearly perfect anapestic phrases:

Не хочу́, чтоб меня́, как цвето́чек с поля́н . . .
Я хочу́, чтоб в деба́тах поте́л Госпла́н . . .
Я хочу́, чтоб над мы́слью времён комисса́р . . .
Я хочу́, чтоб сверхста́вками спе́ца . . .
Я хочу́ чтоб в конце́ рабо́ты завко́м . . .
Я хочу́, чтоб к штыку́ приравня́ли перо́.

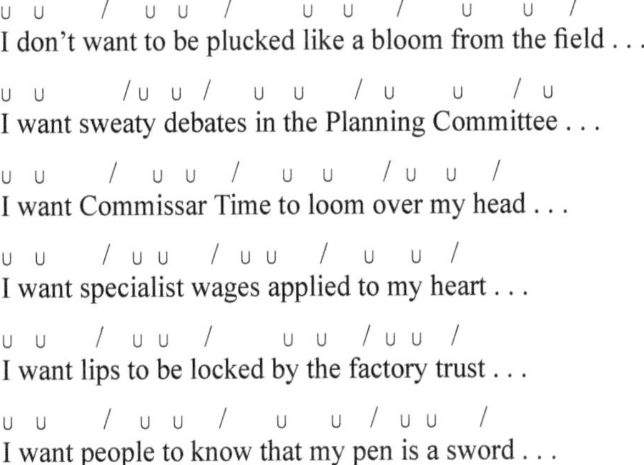

M's usual method of writing was to compose verse as he walked. ("It's this way," he said, "I walk along. And all of the sudden a big desk appears in the air above me.")(1) But here, confined to his cabin, lying listlessly in his bunk, he's at the mercy of the rhythms of the sea below and the and the music above. These external cadences set off an internal stream of thoughts and associations, culminating in an anapestic lament from the depths of his soul: "I want . . . I want . . . I want . . . I want . . . I want . . . I want my country to understand me!"

Обнимись, души и моря глубь/Embrace, depths of soul and sea.

It may seem strange to see a the command to "embrace one another" in 2nd person familiar, but it is a legitimate conjugation. "Глубь" is singular, but it makes no sense in English to say "Embrace one another, depth of soul and sea."

Я в худшей каюте из всех кают/I'm in the worst cabin of all

After his visit to America, M was as broke as he'd ever been in his adult life, and could only afford a 3rd class ticket for his return passage.

Тот, кто постоянно ясен/The one who's always clear

A play on words that sustains the sea imagery of the first lines. "Ясно" is a mark on the Russian barometer indicating clear weather, and also a description of mood—someone who always in high spirits, calm and cloudless.

зачем ты, Маркита, не любишь меня?/Why don't you love me Marquita?

"Homeward" is a poem of unrequited love, and this little tune, which M finds so annoying, is the theme song. The poet throws himself "into communism from the heav-

(1) Helen Muchnic, *From Gorky to Pasternak* (Vintage Books, 1961), 270.

ens of poetry," because without it, "love doesn't exist" for him. But like Marquita, communism doesn't seem to love him back.

From his return from America until his death in 1930, M was in full "Soviet factory" mode, producing poems and articles to fulfill the "social orders" of the party.[(2)] Suppressing the personal and the lyrical, he promoted the party line and harshly criticized any fellow writer who deviated from it. (When Pilnyak, Bulgakov and Zamyatin were at their most vulnerable, he enthusiastically joined in on the attacks).[(3)] In spite of this devotion, M never received that ration of "gigantic love" he craved from the party. Instead, he found himself increasingly isolated. In the mid '20s there were multiple literary factions vying to become the official voice of the party, and one by one the groups founded by M (*LEF*, *New LEF*, and *REF*) were outmaneuvered. By 1930, he had lost the support of both the party and his literary peers.

за сто франков препроводят в кабинет/for 100 francs they'll bring her to your room

"Кабинет" doesn't mean "cabin," although M plays on the identical roots. It's a private office or a separate room in a restaurant where couples can "dine" privately.

будешь всучивать ей швейную машинку/you'll push a sewing machine on her

The reference is to a long-standing tradition, going back to Chernyshevsky, of saving and re-educating the "fallen women." The standard method way of rehabilitating a prostitute was to get her a job as a seamstress.

послан к маме/sent packing

This literally means "sent off to momma," but a much ruder phrase is implied: "послать кого-то на хуй/reject someone; tell someone to fuck off."

чтобы делал доклады Сталин/that Stalin deliver reports

This was 1925, before Stalin had consolidated control of the party, and he appears here only because of his name, which means "Man of Steel." It's convenient for the rhyme "стали/Сталин," and also for the industrial imagery: the steel of words, the brass of bass, a factory of happiness.

---

(2) In "How Are Verses Made?" M wrote that poetry should be a response to the "presence of a problem in society, the solution of which is conceivable only in poetical terms. A social command."

(3) For a concise account, see Jangfeldt, 453-458.

пройду стороной/off to the side

Not "sideways," but rather "on the sidelines." Not being particularly prominent or visible.

Сергею Есенину

Вы ушли́,
как говори́тся,
в мир ино́й.
Пустота́...
Лети́те,
в звёзды врéзываясь.
Ни тебé ава́нса,
ни пивно́й.
Трéзвость.
Нет, Есéнин,
э́то
не насмéшка.
В го́рле
го́ре ко́мом —
не смешо́к.
Ви́жу -
взрéзанной руко́й помéшкав,
со́бственных
костéй
кача́ете мешо́к.
- Прекрати́те!
Бро́сьте!
Вы в своём умé ли?
Дать,
чтоб щёки
залива́л
смертéльный мел?!
Вы ж
тако́е
загиба́ть умéли,
что друго́й
на свéте
не умéл.
Почему́?
Зачéм?
Недоумéнье смя́ло.
Кри́тики бормо́чут:
— Э́тому вина́
то...

To Sergei Esenin

You left,
as they say,
for another world.
Emptiness . . .
You're flying,
crashing into stars.
Neither a writer's advance
nor a pub for you.
Sobriety.
No, Esenin,
this
is not mockery.
The lump in my throat
is grief—
not laughter.
I see you—
hesitating,
swinging a sack
of your own bones
with your slashed arm—
Stop it!
Drop it!
Are you in your right mind?
To allow
death-white chalk
to spread over
your cheeks?
You
could bend words
like
no one
else
on earth.
Why?
What for?
The bewilderment is crushing.
The critics mumble:
"This and that
are

да сё...
а гла́вное,
что смы́чки ма́ло,
в результа́те
мно́го пи́ва и вина́.—
Де́скать,
замени́ть бы вам
боге́му
кла́ссом,
класс влия́л на вас,
и бы́ло б не до драк.
Ну, а класс-то
жа́жду
залива́ет ква́сом?
Класс - он то́же
вы́пить не дура́к.
Де́скать,
к вам приста́вить бы
кого́ из напосто́в —
ста́ли б
содержа́нием
премно́го одарённей.
Вы бы
в день
писа́ли
строк по сто́,
утоми́тельно
и дли́нно,
как Доро́нин.
А по-мо́ему,
осуществи́сь
така́я бредь,
на себя́ бы
ра́ньше наложи́ли ру́ки.
Лу́чше уж
от во́дки умере́ть,
чем от ску́ки!
Не откро́ют
нам
причи́н поте́ри
ни петля́,

to blame…
but above all,
not enough guidance from the proletariat,
resulting
in a lot of beer and wine."
They say,
if you'd replaced
your Bohemian circle
with the proletariat,
the class would have influenced you,
you wouldn't have felt like brawling.
Maybe, but does the working class
quench
its thirst with kvass?
The proletariat is no fool
when it comes to drinking.
They say,
if we had appointed someone from *On Guard*
to look after you—
your content
would have become
much richer.
You would have
written
a hundred lines
a day,
wearisome
and lengthy
like Doronin.
Well, I think
if they had accomplished
this kind of rubbish,
you would have
laid hands on yourself even earlier.
Better
to die from vodka
than from boredom!
Neither the noose
nor your penknife
will reveal
the cause of this loss.

ни нóжик перочи́нный.
Мóжет,
окажи́сь
черни́ла в «Англетéре»,
вéны
рéзать
нé было б причи́ны.
Подражáтели обрáдовались:
бис!
Над собóю
чуть не взвод
распрáву учини́л.
Почемý же
увели́чивать
чи́сло самоуби́йств?
Лýчше
увели́чь
изготовлéние черни́л!
Навсегдá
тепéрь
язы́к
в зубáх затвóрится.
Тяжелó
и неумéстно
разводи́ть мистéрии.
У нарóда,
у языкотвóрца,
ýмер
звóнкий
забулды́га подмастéрье.
И несýт
стихóв заупокóйный лом,
с прóшлых
с похорóн
не передéлавши почти́.
В холм
тупы́е ри́фмы
загоня́ть колóм —
рáзве так
поэ́та
нáдо бы почти́ть?

to us.
Maybe
if some ink
had turned up at the "Angleterre"
there wouldn't have been any reason
to cut open
your veins.
Your imitators were elated:
encore!
Nearly a platoon of them
has inflicted
this cruelty upon themselves.
Why
increase
the number of suicides?
Better
to increase
the production of ink!
Now
your tongue
is locked behind your teeth
forever.
It's distressing
and wrong
to turn this into a mystery play.
The people,
the master craftsmen of language,
have lost
a sonorous
and dissolute apprentice.
And they're bringing
funereal scraps of poetry,
barely altered
from earlier
funerals.
Driving
insipid rhymes
into the fresh earth of your grave—
is this how
you honor
a poet?

Вам
        и па́мятник ещё не слит,-
где он,
        бро́нзы звон,
                или грани́та грань? —
а к решёткам па́мяти
                уже́
                        понанесли́
посвяще́ний
        и воспомина́ний дрянь.
Ва́ше и́мя
        в плато́чки рассо́плено,
ва́ше сло́во
        слюня́вит Со́бинов
и выво́дит
        под берёзкой до́хлой -
«Ни сло́ва,
        о дру-уг мой,
                ни вздо-о́-о-о-ха.»
Эх,
    поговори́ть бы и́наче
с э́тим са́мым
        с Леони́дом Лоэнгри́нычем!
Встать бы здесь
        гремя́щим скандали́стом:
- Не позво́лю
        мя́млить стих
                и мять!-
Оглуши́ть бы
        их
            трёхпа́лым сви́стом
в ба́бушку
        и в бо́га ду́шу мать!
Что́бы разнесла́сь
        безда́рнейшая по́гань,
раздува́я
        темь
            пиджа́чных парусо́в,
что́бы
    врассыпну́ю
            разбежа́лся Ко́ган,

Your monument
hasn't been cast yet—
where is it,
the ring of bronze
or the facet of granite?—
but the garbage of dedications
and reminiscences
has already been delivered
to the railings
of your memory.
Your name
blown and wiped into hankies,
Sobinov slobbers
your words
under a dead birch tree
and draws out —
"Not a word,
oh fri-e-end of mine,
not a si-i-i-i-gh."
Oh,
I'd like to have a different sort of talk
with this very same
Leonid Lohengrin!
I'd stand up
and make a scene:
"I won't let you
drawl out a verse
and mangle it!"
I'd like to deafen
them
with a three-fingered whistle
"Go screw your grandmother
and goddamn mother too!"
So that talentless filth
would scatter,
puffing up
the blackness
of their coat jacket sails,
so that Kogan
would run like crazy
in every direction,

встре́ченных
увéча
пи́ками усóв.
Дрянь
покá что
мáло поредéла.
Дéла мнóго —
тóлько поспевáть.
Нáдо
жизнь
сначáла передéлать,
передéлав —
мóжно воспевáть.
Э́то врéмя —
трудновáто для перá,
но скажи́те
вы,
калéки и калéкши,
где,
когдá,
какóй вели́кий выбирáл
путь,
чтóбы протóптанней
и лéгше?
Слóво -
полковóдец
человéчьей си́лы.
Марш!
Чтоб врéмя
сзáди
я́драми рвалóсь.
К стáрым дням
чтоб вéтром
относи́ло
тóлько
пу́таницу волóс.
Для весéлия
планéта нáша
мáло обору́дована.
Нáдо
вы́рвать

mutilating
passersby
with his mustache lances.
For now
this trash
hasn't thinned out much.
There's a lot to do—
we just need to get ready.
Life
needs to be
refashioned.
Once it's refashioned—
we can sing praises.
These times
are difficult for the pen,
but tell me,
you
cripples and cripplettes,
where,
when,
what great being chose
a path,
because it was well-traveled
and easy?
The word
is a commander
of human forces.
March!
So that time
would explode like cannon balls
behind us
So the wind
would carry away
only
a tangle of hair
to the old days.
Our planet
is ill equipped
for merry-making.
We have to
tear

ра́дость

у гряду́щих дней.

В э́той жи́зни

помере́ть

не тру́дно.

Сде́лать жизнь

значи́тельно трудне́й.

1926

our happiness
from future days.
In this life
it's not hard
to die.
To build a life
is considerably harder.

Сергею Есенину/To Sergei Esenin

Sergei Esenin, the most popular poet in Russia next to Pushkin, committed suicide in a Leningrad hotel room at the age of 30. Between slashing his wrists and hanging himself on a water pipe, he managed to write a farewell poem in his own blood, which appeared in the newspapers the next morning:

До свиданья, друг мой, до свиданья. Милый мой, ты у меня в груди. Предназначенное расставанье Обещает встречу впереди.	Goodbye, my friend, goodbye. My dear one, you're in my heart. This predetermined parting promises a reunion ahead.
До свиданья, друг мой, без руки, без слова, Не грусти и не печаль бровей,- В этой жизни умирать не ново, Но и жить, конечно, не новей.	Goodbye, my friend, without a handshake, without a word. Don't be sad and don't furrow your brow. In this life, dying isn't new, Though living, of course, isn't any newer.

"After these lines," wrote Mayakovsky, "Esenin's death became a literary fact. It was clear at once how many insecure people these powerful lines, just these lines of poetry, could bring to the rope or the revolver. And no amount of analysis in the newspapers, no amount of articles, can wipe out these lines. One can and must combat these verses only with verses."(1) M took up this task and struggled mightily for several months to formulate a response which would "neutralize the effect of Esenin's last lines, to make Esenin's death uninteresting, to replace the facile beauty of death by another beauty." The result was this poem, which M considered to be one of his best.

Ни тебе аванса/No advance for you

Six months before his death, Esenin signed a contract with Gosizdat, the state publishing house, receiving the unheard of rate of 1 ruble a line for a large collection of poems. On top of that he tried to negotiate a 2000-ruble advance for the book (and nearly succeeded). M, who himself was paid a mere 12 kopecks a line for his own collected works, was understandably upset by this.

ни пивной/no bar

Esenin was a notorious drunk, and towards the end of his life, as Mayakovsky reported, "one came across him more often in police records than in poetry."

---

(1) "How Are Verses Made?", Carrick, 241.

щёки заливал смертельный мел/deathly chalk filled your cheeks
A combination of two set phrases, "белый как мел/white as chalk" and "белый как смерть/pale as death."

смычки мало/Smichka was insufficient
Smichka is a Soviet term for the union of the proletariat and peasantry. At the time of the 1917 revolution, Russia was 80% agrarian, which did not reconcile with Marxist theory—communist revolutions were supposed to happen in industrialized nations. So Lenin came up with the idea of smichka as a theoretical justification. In this union the proletariat, as the carrier of the correct socialist ideology, was supposed to lead and educate the peasants. The peasants did not fare well in this relationship, enduring repeated and persistent abuse at the hands of their supposed benefactors.(2) The notion that a proletarian with the proper class view could have "guided" Esenin, who was of peasant origin himself, seems not only absurd, but insulting.

M is clearly mocking these "mumbling" critics with their post mortem prescriptions, but there is a level of self-contradiction. In *How Are Verses Made?*, he himself wrote that a true devotion to the revolution might have saved Esenin. He also propagandized the idea of smichka: in the 1923 poem "Смыкай ряды/Close the ranks" he calls for the "unbreakable union of worker and peasant," and urges the peasants to share their harvest with the cities.

классом/class
The proletariat class at large.

Квас/Kvass
Kvass is a traditional fermented drink with a very low alcohol content—the Russian equivalent of a soft drink.

кого из напостов/someone from *On Guard*
"Напостовцы/Napostovsi" were members of the leftist journal *On Guard,* who advocated class principles in literature and aggressively attacked other writers, including Mayakovsky himself, for not being truly proletarian.

(2) In M's lifetime, multiple representatives of the proletariat (the Red Army, political activists, the Komsomol, brigades of urban workers, and the NKVD) came to the villages requisition grain, to collect taxes, to destroy churches, to seize livestock, land and equipment, to arrest, deport and execute the "kulaks," and to forceably conscript reluctant peasants into collective farms.

стали б содержанием премного одарённей/your content would have become much richer
In other words, "your writing would have gained in 'class' content"—it would have been more expressive of proletarian ideology.

Над собою чуть не взвод расправу учинил/nearly a platoon has committed this same atrocity.
Esenin's death was followed by a rash of copycat suicides: a former lover even shot her herself in the heart at his graveside.

неуместно разводить мистерии/It's inappropriate to make this into a mystery play
M himself wrote *Mystery-Bouffe*, a comedy which presented the revolution in the format of a medieval religious play. But the allusion may be to the more ancient mystery rites as associated with Dionysus or, more appropriately, Orpheus.

У народа, у языкотворца, умер звонкий забулдыга подмастерье/The people, the craftsmen of language, have lost a sonorous and dissolute apprentice
M is touching on an old and familiar theme—that the true creator of the Russian language was the peasantry. Esenin was a rare realization of this idea: countless writers idolized the peasant as an embodiment of the Russian soul, wrote from the peasants' point of view, were inspired by peasant speech, by peasant tales, songs, curses and proverbs, but none were peasants themselves. Born into a family of Old Believers and raised in the countryside of Ryazan, Esenin could rightly claim to be a genuine poet of the people. He wrote gorgeous and intimate poems about village life, about nature, and, as he spiraled into alcoholism, about his drunken encounters with prostitutes, thieves and brawlers in the taverns of Moscow. There's nothing theoretical, technically brilliant or innovative about his poetry, and if it's sometimes hard to understand, it's only because his imagery is so strong that language can't seem to contain it. Both in style and content he's the polar opposite of Mayakovsky. Among M's contemporaries there were many great poets—Blok, Mandelstam, Akhmatova, Tsvetaeva, Pasternak—but his primary rival was Esenin. What M so desperately sought his whole career—to be loved and understood by the Russian people—was something Esenin achieved organically and effortlessly.

В холм тупые рифмы загонять колом/driving dull rhymes into your grave with a stake
"Холм" is a burial mound (могильный холм). Perhaps the image is of placing spadefuls of earth on the grave, but in a painful manner that doesn't allow the deceased to rest in peace.

Собинов/Sobinov

Leonid Sobinov, a Russian tenor. Esenin's death inspired an outpouring of poems, articles, reminiscences, essays and even theatrical performances. At one of these events Sobinov sang a sentimental tribute under a prop birch, which M found particularly offensive.

с Леонидом Лоэнгринычем/with Leonid Sobinov

The same Leonid Sobinov, who was famous for his performances in Wagner's opera *Lohengrin*. M is using the opera's name as Sobinov's patronymic.

Оглушить бы их трёхпалым свистом/(I'd) deafen them with a 3-fingered whistle

It's natural to assume that the speaker here is Mayakovsky, but since the subject isn't named (there's no "I"), but it's possible that this is actually supposed to be Esenin. Esenin wrote several poems where the hero rudely whistles.

в бога душу мать/screw your mother

This is a milder, verbless version of "ёб твою мать/fuck your mother."

Коган/Kogan

P.S. Kogan, a Marxist literary critic, who, like the writer Ivan Doronin, is remembered today only because of his appearance in this poem. Mayakovsky never hesitated to use his verse as a platform to publically humiliate his contemporaries, immortalizing these "unworthy opponents and literary hacks," to quote Dmity Bykov, "like flies in the amber of his poetic testament."(3)

Сделать жизнь значительно трудней/To create a life is much harder

The last lines of the poem are an inversion of and direct response to Esenin's suicide poem. They are also an expression of M's artistic philosophy, "Constructivism." The Constructivists rejected the idea of "art for art's sake." The purpose of art was to serve production (allowing the natural properties of materials to determine form rather than some egotistical artistic vision), and for production to serve the people. The aim of Constructivism was purely utilitarian: to aid the state in the building of the new Soviet society.

(3) Bykov, 761.

Разгово́р на Оде́сском ре́йде деса́нтных судо́в

Пе́рья-облака́,
зака́т расканаре́йте!
Опуска́йся,
ю́жной но́чи гнёт!
Па́ра
пароxо́дов
говори́т на ре́йде:
то оди́н моргнёт,
а то
друго́й моргнёт.
Что сигна́лят?
Напряга́ю я
морщи́ны лба.
Кра́сный раз...
уга́снет,
и зелёный...
Мо́жет быть,
любо́вная мольба́.
Мо́жет быть,
ревну́ет разозлённый.
Мо́жет, про́сит:
— «Кра́сная Абха́зия»!
Говори́т
«Сове́тский Дагеста́н».
Я уста́л,
оди́н по мо́рю ла́зая,
Подойди́ сюда́
и ря́дом стань.-
Но в отве́т
кова́рная
она́:
— Как-нибу́дь
оди́н
живи́ и гре́йся.
Я
тепе́рь
по ма́чты влюблена́
в се́рый «Коминте́рн»,
трёхтру́бный кре́йсер.

A conversation between landing craft in the Odessa Port

Feather-clouds,
un-yellow the sunset!
Settle in,
weight of southern night!
A pair
of steamships
talk in the port:
now one winks,
and then
another one.
What are they signaling?
I'm straining
every wrinkle on my brow.
One red blink . . .
it will fade away,
then a green one.
Maybe
a lover's plea.
Maybe
a jealous hothead.
Maybe he's asking:
"Red Abkhazia!
This is
'Soviet Dagestan!'
I'm tired
of crawling along the sea alone.
Come over here
and stand next to me."
But the treacherous
female
replies:
"You'll have to
live and make do
on your own.
I'm
now
in love up to my masts
with grey 'Komintern,'
a three-stack cruiser."

— Все вы,
бáбы,
трясогýзки и канáльи...
Что ей крéйсер,
ды́лда и пачкýн? —
Поскули́л
и снóва засигнáлил:
- Ктó-нибудь,
пришли́те табачкý!..
Скýчно здесь,
нехорошó
и мóкро.
Здесь
от скýки
отсырéет и броня́... —
Дрéмлет мир,
на Черномóрский óкруг
синь-слези́щу
мóрем оброня́.

1926

"All of you
women
are wagtails and deceivers. . ."
What does she see in a cruiser,
that string bean, that bum?
He whined for a while
and started signaling again.
"Someone
send over some tobacco!
It's bad here,
boring
and wet.
Even my armor
is getting
damp here from boredom."
The world is dozing,
letting an immense blue tear
well up on the Odessa province
as the sea.

Разговор на Одесском рейде десантных судов/A conversation in the Odessa Port between landing craft

In *I Myself*, Mayakovsky describes 1926 as a year of non-stop travel:

> "…continued the broken-off tradition of the troubadours and minstrels. Toured cities and gave readings. Novocherkassk, Vinnitsa, Kharkov, Paris, Rostov, Tblisi, Berlin, Kazan, Sverdlovsk, Tula, Prague, Leningrad, Moscow, Voronezh, Yalta, Yevpatoria, Vyatka, Ufa, etc., etc., etc." (1)

Like the steamship Dagestan, Mayakovsky seemed to have a love interest in every port—Ellie Jones in New York, his old flame Elsa Kagan (later Elsa Troilet) in Paris, Natasha Xhmelnitsa in Kharkov, Natalya Ryabova in Kiev, Natasha Briukhanenko in Moscow, etc., etc., etc. His Odessa girlfriend, for one week in the summer of 1926, was a poetry lover named Zhenya Dyakanova. M spotted her from his hotel balcony, sitting across the street holding one of his books in her hands. They exchanged looks, M lifted his wineglass to her and then came down to introduce himself, using one of his standard pick-up lines. "Comrade Miss! You're just my size. Let's take a walk together." (Another tried and true gambit—"Comrade Miss! Do you like poetry?" followed by "Who's your favorite poet?")

They spent several evenings together in the port of Odessa, boarding the ships there, talking to the sailors, and taking turns reciting poetry, sometimes all night long. "A Conversation" was inspired by these evenings. It's one of M's most touching poems—a lonely ship longing for love is met with indifference from the "treacherous female," and has to settle instead for a little tobacco.(2)

десантных судов/landing craft
Though the poem is supposed to be about landing craft, there are none—only cruisers and steamships.

закат расканарейте/un-yellow the sunset
Literally "un-canary" the sunset.

Опускайся/Settle in
In this context, "опускайся" doesn't really mean "come down," but refers to the general onset/gathering of the darkness.

---

(1) McGavran, 29.

(2) This account is from taken from Bykov, "Odesskoe Schast'e" 666-682.

Все вы, бабы, трясогузки и канальи.../All of you women are wagtails and scoundrels

The official definition of "баба" is "a married peasant woman," but it's a mildly derogatory term for women in general. "Трясогузка" is a small bird in the sparrow family, distinguished by its constantly twitching long narrow tail. It also means a "fidgety, delicately built woman"—a flighty and fickle female. It's also the poem's third bird reference ("feather cloud," "un-canary").

Письмó товáрищу Кострóву из Парúжа о сýщности любвú

Простúте
меня́,
товáрищ Кострóв,
с присýщей
душéвной шúрью,
что часть
на Парúж отпýщенных строф
на лúрику
я
растранжúрю.
Представьте:
вхóдит
красáвица в зал,
в мехá
и бýсы опрáвленная.
Я
э́ту красáвицу взял
и сказáл:
- прáвильно сказáл
или непрáвильно? —
Я, товáрищ,-
из Россúи,
знаменúт в своéй странé я,
я видáл
девúц красúвей,
я видáл
девúц стройнéе.
Дéвушкам
поэ́ты лю́бы.
Я ж умён
и голосúст,
заговáриваю зýбы —
тóлько
слýшать согласúсь.
Не поймáть
меня́
на дря́ни,
на прохóжей

A letter to Comrade Kostrov from Paris on the nature of love

Forgive
me,
Comrade Kostrov,
with the natural
generosity of your soul
for
squandering
part
of the stanzas allotted to Paris
on love poetry.
Imagine:
a beautiful woman
enters the hall
framed
in fur and jewels.
I
took this beauty
and said
—did I say it right
or wrong?—
I, comrade,
am from Russia,
I'm well known in my country,
I've seen
girls who are more beautiful,
I've seen
girls with better figures.
Girls
love poets.
And I'm intelligent
and loud-mouthed.
I'm a smooth talker
if only
you'll agree to listen.
I won't fall
for something
cheap
Or be ensnared on a passing

пáре чувств.
Я ж
навéк
любóвью рáнен —
éле-éле волочýсь.
Мне
любóвь
не свáдьбой мéрить:
разлюбúла -
уплылá.
Мне, товáрищ,
в вы́сшей мéре
наплевáть
на куполá.
Что ж в подрóбности вдавáться,
шýтки брóсьте-ка,
мне ж, красáвица,
не двáдцать, —
трúдцать...
с хвóстиком.
Любóвь
не в том,
чтоб кипéть крутéй,
не в том,
что жгут ýгольями,
а в том,
что встаёт за горáми грудéй
над
волосáми-джýнглями.
Любúть -
это знáчит:
в глубь дворá
вбежáть
и до ночи грáчьей,
блестя́ топорóм,
рубúть дровá,
сúлой
своéй
игрáючи.
Любúть —
э́то с прóстынь,

pair of feelings.
I've already
been wounded by love
for good—
just barely dragging myself around.
I'm not one
to measure love
by marriage:
she could fall out of love
and swim away.
I, comrade,
don't give a
supreme damn
about church domes.
Why go into details,
Let's stop joking around,
After all, beautiful lady,
I'm not twenty—
but thirty . . .
and then some.
Love
isn't about
boiling more forcefully,
or
being burned with hot coals.
It's what
emerges past hills of breasts
above
hair-jungles.
Love—
it means
running
into the depth of the yard
to chop wood,
flashing an ax,
until night's darkest hour,
effortlessly giving play
to one's
strength.
Love
is leaping out of bed

бессо́нницей
рва́ных,
срыва́ться,
ревну́я к Копе́рнику,
его́,
а не му́жа Ма́рьи Ива́нны,
счита́я
свои́м
сопе́рником.
Нам
любо́вь
не рай да ку́щи,
нам
любо́вь
гуди́т про то,
что опя́ть
в рабо́ту пу́щен
се́рдца
вы́стывший мото́р.
Вы
к Москве́
порва́ли нить.
Го́ды -
расстоя́ние.
Как бы
вам бы
объясни́ть
это состоя́ние?
На земле́
огне́й — до не́ба...
В си́нем не́бе
звёзд —
до чёрта.
Е́сли бы я
поэ́том не́ был,
я б
стал бы
звездочётом.
Подыма́ет пло́щадь шум,
экипа́жи дви́жутся,
я хожу́,

away from sheets
lacerated
from sleeplessness,
jealous of Copernicus,
seeing him,
and not Maria Ivanovna's husband,
as
your
rival.
Our
love
isn't heaven or arbors,
for us
love
hums that
the stalled motor
of the heart
is put to work
again.
You
cut the thread
to Moscow
Years—
distance.
How can I
explain
this situation
to you?
On earth
lights reach up to heaven
in the dark blue sky
there are a hell
of a lot of stars.
If I wasn't
a poet
I'd
be
a stargazer.
The square raises a fuss,
carriages bounce along,
I'm walking,

стишки́ пишу́
в записну́ю кни́жицу.
Мчат
авто́
по у́лице,
а не сва́лят на́земь.
Понима́ют
у́мницы:
челове́к —
в экста́зе.
Сонм виде́ний
и иде́й
по́лон
до кры́шки.
Тут бы
и у медведе́й
вы́росли бы кры́лышки.
И вот
с ка́кой-то
грошо́вой столо́вой,
когда́
докипе́ло э́то,
из зе́ва
до звёзд
взвива́ется сло́во
золоторождённой коме́той.
Распла́стан
хвост
небеса́м на треть,
блести́т
и гори́т опере́нье его́,
чтоб двум влюблённым
на звёзды смотре́ть
из и́хней
бесе́дки сире́невой.
Чтоб подыма́ть,
и вести́,
и влечь,
кото́рые гла́зом осла́бли.
Чтоб вра́жьи
го́ловы

writing little verses
in my little note book.
Automobiles
tear
along the street,
but don't knock me down.
They're clever enough
to understand:
this man
is in ecstasy.
A crowd of visions
and ideas
is full
to the lid.
Given this
even bears
could sprout wings.
And so
in some
cheap dining-hall,
when
this has reached a boil,
a word whirls up
from my gullet
to the stars
like a golden-born comet.
Its tail
spread out over
a third of the sky,
its plumage
flashes and burns,
so that two lovers
can look at the stars
from their
lilac arbor.
To raise
and guide
and pull
those with weakened eyes.
To saw
enemy heads

спи́ливать с плеч
хвоста́той
сия́ющей са́блей.
Себя́
до после́днего сту́ка в груди́,
как на свида́нье,
проста́ивая,
прислу́шиваюсь:
любо́вь загуди́т —
челове́ческая,
проста́я.
Урага́н,
ого́нь,
вода́
подступа́ют в ро́поте.
Кто
суме́ет совлада́ть?
Мо́жете?
Попро́буйте...

1928

off from shoulders
with a shining sabre
tail.
As for me,
until the last beat in my chest,
standing aimlessly,
as if on my way to a rendezvous,
I listen
for love to start humming—
human,
simple love,
A hurricane,
fire,
water
approach in a roar.
Who
can control it?
You?
Go ahead and try…

Письмо товарищу Кострову/A letter to comrade Kostrov

In the fall of 1928 M again traveled to France in the capacity of Soviet correspondent, tasked with sending back dispatches on the lives and conditions of young people in Europe. While in Paris, he met the the 22-year-old Russian émigré Tatiana Yakovleva and fell madly in love. Taras Kostrov, the editor of *Young Guard*, could not have been pleased when, instead of the expected socio-economic piece, he received this impassioned love poem. When published, "A letter" set off a storm: How could M, the self-proclaimed poet of the "working and peasant masses"(1) write on such a bourgeois topic? Even worse, the poem was inspired by a "White" Russian,(2) and a Chanel model to boot—not an ideal match for an official representative of the Soviet proletariat.

с присущей душевной ширью/with the inherent kindness of your soul
This is a stock phrase, which might appear in any official letter.

правильно сказал или неправильно/Rightly said or not?
This is an aside to comrade Kostrov.

в меха и бусы оправленная/framed in fur and beads
There's no good translation for "бусы" which has a different connotation in Russian than English. It doesn't necessarily mean beads: she's wearing a long necklace with some kind of precious stones, maybe pearls.

заговариваю зубы/I'm a smooth talker
An idiomatic phrase, meaning to talk a lot, with the intent of diverting the listener from the real issue at hand: "to talk circles around."

Не поймать меня на дряни, на прохожей паре чувств/You won't catch me with trash, with a pair of passing feelings
A freer translation would be "I won't fall for cheap romance."

---

(1) From M's *Address at the Krasnaya Presnya Komsomol Club*: ". . .the poet of the old days who was read and listened to by 'young ladies' and 'young men' in smart salons is dead forever and only the working-class auditorium, only the proletariat masses, those that are now building our new life, are fit listeners and readers, and I can only be the poet of these people." Carrick, 268.

(2) T. Yakovleva was from a well-to-do St. Petersburg family, and emigrated to France after the Russian Civil War.

разлюбила – уплыла/She'd fall out of love and swim away

Another nice example of fluidity of verb tense in Russian. Although "разлюбила" and "уплыла" are in past perfective, the meaning is subjunctive.

Любить—это значит /Love means . . .

As Dmitry Bykov has pointed out, this famous declaration of love is evocative of the scene from *Fathers and Sons* where Bazarov, tormented by his love for Anna Odintsova, strides off into the woods and furiously breaks off the twigs and branches that appear in his path.[(3)] This motif of impassioned lover vs. plant matter also occurs in *Oblomov*, where the hero tears up a bush with his bare hands—it blocks Olga's view from the pavilion.

до ночи грачьей/until the darkest hour of the night

Literally, "until the raven's night," meaning "until night is black as a raven."

играючи/As if child's play

He's so energized by love that he swings the ax like a toy.

На земле огней - до неба... В синем небе звёзд - до чёрта/On earth light reach the sky . . . in heaven there are a hell of a lot of stars

A play on words: both "до неба/to heaven" and "до чёрта/to the devil" mean "a lot of."

из зева до звёзд/from my gullet to the stars

Another play on words, as the sounds of "зев" and "звезда" are very similar, but the meanings are very different.

простаивая/stalled

This is only used in reference to equipment that has stopped working.

(3) Bykov, 738.

Расска́з Хре́нова о Кузне́цкстро́е и о лю́дях Кузне́цка

К этому месту будет подвезено в пятилетку 1 000 000 вагонов строительных материалов. Здесь будет гигант металлургии, угольный гигант и город в сотни тысяч людей.

Из разговора.

По не́бу
ту́чи бе́гают,
дождя́ми
су́мрак сжат,
под ста́рою
теле́гою
рабо́чие лежа́т.
И слы́шит
шёпот го́рдый
вода́
и под
и над:
«Чере́з четы́ре
го́да
здесь
бу́дет
го́род-сад!»
Темно́ свинцовоно́чие,
и до́ждик
толст, как жгут,
сидя́т
в грязи́
рабо́чие,
сидя́т,
лучи́ну жгут.
Сливе́ют
гу́бы
с хо́лода,
но гу́бы
ше́пчут в лад:
«Чере́з четы́ре
года
здесь
бу́дет

Khrenov's story about Kuznetsk-construction and the people of Kuznetsk

There will be 1,000,000 wagons of construction material brought to this site. There will be a giant metallurgical plant, a giant coal mine and a city for hundreds of thousands.

From a conversation.

Clouds are running
along the sky,
twilight is squeezed
with rain,
workers are lying
under an old
wagon.
The water
above
and below
hears
the proud whisper:
"In four
years from now
there'll be
a garden-city
here!"
The leaden clouds are dark as night,
and the rain is thick
as plaits,
the worker
sit
in the mud,
they sit,
and light kindling sticks.
Their lips
turn purple
from cold,
but their lips
whisper in unison:
"In four
years from now
there'll be
a garden-city

гóрод-сад!»
Свелá
промóзглость
кóрчею —
невáжный
мокр
уют,
сидят
впотьмáх
рабóчие,
подмóкший
хлеб
жуют.
Но шёпот
грóмче гóлода —
он крóет
кáпель
спад:
«Черéз четыре
гóда
здесь
бýдет
гóрод-сад!»
Здесь
взрывы закудáхтают
в разгóн
медвéжьих банд,
и взрóет
нéдра
шáхтою
стоýгольный
«Гигáнт».
Здесь
встáнут
стрóйки
стéнами.
Гудкáми,
пар,
сипи.
Мы
в сóтню солнц

here!”
Everyone
is cramped
in the dankness.
The comforts
are lousy
and wet,
the workers
sit
in the dark,
chewing
their
sodden bread.
But their whisper
is louder than hunger--
it drowns out
the fall
of rain:
“In four
years from now
there’ll be
a garden-city
here!”
Explosions
will start cackling here
bear gangs
will scatter,
And the super coal mine
“the Giant”
will plough up
the bowels
of the earth.
Construction sites
will rise up
here
in walls.
Steam!
Hiss
through your sirens.
We’ll
set Siberia

мартéнами
воспламени́м
Сиби́рь.
Здесь дом
дадýт
хорóший нам
и си́тный
без пайкá,
аж за Байкáл
отбрóшенная
попя́тится тайгá.
Рос
шепотóк рабóчего
над тéмью
тýчных стад,
а дáльше
неразбóрчиво
лишь слы́шно —
«гóрод-сад».
Я знáю —
гóрод
бýдет,
я знáю —
сáду
цвесть,
когдá
таки́е лю́ди
в странé
в совéтской
есть!

1929

ablaze
in a hundred suns
with furnaces.
They'll give
us
good lodging
and good bread
with no rationing,
the taiga
will be pushed back,
and retreat even beyond Baikal.
The worker's whisper
rose
above masses
of dark clouds,
and farther
barely discernable,
were the the words
"garden-city."
I know
there will be
a city,
I know
a garden
will bloom,
when
there are people like this
in
our Soviet
land!

Рассказ Хренова о Кузнецкстрое и о людях Кузнецка/Khrenov's Story about Kuznetsk-construction and the People of Kuznetsk

The first Soviet five year plan (1928-1933) called for the construction of industrial cities across the country. The coal-rich Kuznetsk Basin in Western Siberia was the location of one of these massive complexes. By the summer of 1931, as predicted, there was indeed "a giant metallurgical plant, a giant coal mine, and a city for hundreds of thousands" by the banks of the Tom River. The "garden-city" of Novokuznetsk has been a major producer of coal, iron, steel and aluminum from the '30s to this day, and played a crucial role in WWII, supplying the Soviet military with millions of tons of the raw material needed for its heavy weaponry.

M's dedication to the Kuznetsk-construction project and its workers is one of 200 plus propaganda pieces he churned out during the late 20s. Many of the poems in this genre are painful to read. Some are bullying: he calls out fellow writers by name and advises them to embrace a socialist agenda, he demands that peasants adopt modern farming methods, he rails against the domestic comforts of "Soviet philistines." Some are condescending: peasants and workers marvel at the technical advances of socialism (lightbulbs, radios, an indoor bath with hot and cold running water). Some are corny: "the thing we cherish the most, which will never be outshadowed, is our Soviet Land, gaining daily in might, our Soviet freedom, and our Soviet sunshine, our Soviet banner." Or "My land is young and special. It's free to imagine, create and be brave! Gladness gushes. Would you like a bucketful?" And some are cringeworthy: marches for shock brigades heading off to the villages to force peasants into collective farms, a poem dedicated to "The Soldiers of Dzerzhensky" (i.e. the NKVD), a poem condemning "saboteurs," written on the occasion of the Shakhy trail.(1)

M himself recognized that he was doing hackwork (as he told the artist Yury Annenkov in 1928, "I have already stopped being a poet. Nowadays I am. . . a functionary.").(2) But "Khrenov's story" is an exception: M's admiration for the people of Kuznetsk is real, and it's this respectful tone, along with the frank (if not full) acknowledgment of the harsh working conditions, that makes this such an effective piece of propaganda. The tone is achieved through a rare feat—beyond some of the usual stylistic markers (neologisms, *lensenka* format, word play), M has kept his own persona completely out the poem. The focus is entirely on the workers, on their suffering and heroism,

(1) In 1928 a national campaign against saboteurs began with a show trial: 56 mining engineers were accused of working with foreigners to disrupt production. Confessions were extracted by torture, 11 of the defendants were sentenced to death, the rest sent to prison.

(2) Jangfeldt, 434.

and the voice is theirs. And the voice is effective—the poem has all the build, sustain, and take-off of a great pop song. The speech is simple and straightforward, delivered in the most common of meters, iambic tetrameter. The verses enumerate the workers' woes—"the water above and below," the cold, the dark; the chorus expresses their shining hope—"Four years from now we'll have a garden-city!" Three rounds of verse/chorus are followed by a bridge declaring the vision's achievement (explosions, a mine ploughing up the earth, construction sites rising up, sirens, smelting ovens, and finally—food and shelter). Then comes the grand finale—a rousing declaration of confidence in the Soviet worker. "I know there will be a city, I know a garden will bloom, when there are people like this in our country, in our Soviet land!.

According to Soviet sources, the poem was very effective in its ability to inspire disheartened workers:

> "The poem written by Mayakovsky reached the construction workers of Kuznetsk. The writer Alexander Smerdov, who was a there as a reporter, recalled what a mobilizing effect the poetic verses of Mayakovsky had: 'One of our fitters read Mayakovsky's poem to the builders during the days when the concrete foundation for the first blast furnace was being prepared. It had become so cold that the workers couldn't mix the concrete before it turned into stone, but the bricklayers were going ahead and laying the foundation. Carpenters were trying to cover the construction sites, but the blizzard was determined to whisk them away from the scaffolding, frost had permeated the iron, so that that the palms of the fitters stuck to it and froze, but the carpenters kept raising the scaffolding, the fitters kept bending the iron rods and weaving the framework of the factory. The comrades in the brigade began to complain about the frost, but the fitter Volodya, a Komsomol member, in a voice hoarse from the cold, shouted out the verses of Mayakovsky: "Their lips turn blue from cold, but their lips whisper in harmony: In four years from now there'll be a garden city here!" [(3)]

город-сад a 'garden-city.'
The design of Novokuznetsk was inspired by the urban planning ideas of Sir Ebenezer Howard, author of *Garden Cities of To-morrow* (1902). The city is laid in a half-circle with radial boulevards, and has plenty of parks, fountains and open squares (one featuring a statue of Mayakovsky!). And though, as prescribed, the city has well-defined zones for urban life, housing, and industry, with a carefully planned

(3) B. Chelyshev, *Poiski, vstrechi, nakhodki.* (Kemerovskoe knizhnoe izdatel'stvo, 1963), 23 (as cited in Kovalenko, S. A. Kommentarii k stikhotvoreniyu V. V. Mayakovskogo, http://v-v-mayakovsky.ru/books/item/f00/s00/z0000006/st046.shtml, accessed Sept. 2017).

mix of greenery, the moniker "garden-city" is a sad joke—Novokuznetsk is one of the most polluted cities in all of Russia (right now ranking #3).

Из разговора/from a conversation

The poem was inspired by a conversation M had in the fall of 1929 with the engineer Julian P. Khrenov. While serving on the Central Counsel for the Union of Metalworkers, Khrenov was deployed to Kuznetskstroy to help with the construction of the metallurgical combine. The artist Nikolay Denisovsky remembered: "I met Julian Petrovich Khrenov at V.V. Mayakovsky's apartment, who was very fond of him. Mayakovsky appreciated his enthusiasm, boundless energy and devotion to his entrusted task. . . Khrenov had just returned from the Kuznetsk Basin and told some very interesting stories about the feats of the people of Kuznetskstroy. . ." (4)

In 1936 Khrenov was arrested for "counter-revolutionary Trotskyist activities" and sent to the Artic Circle to work in the mines of Kolyma. On the same prison transport ship was the writer Varlam Sharlamov, who, in his memoirs, recalled that out of the thousands of prisoners in the hold, Khrenov was the only one carrying a book with him. The book was a single volume of Mayakovsky, which included the poem "Khrenov's story."

Khrenov actually survived his 5-year prison sentence, and worked as a mining chief in Siberia until his death from heart disease in 1946.

вода и под и над/water above and below

To his credit, M does not sugar coat the miserable conditions at Kuznetskstroy. Even though Khrenov, a committed party member, surely self-censored his "interesting stories," the basic facts come through: the workers had little protection from the elements, lacked simple tools, and suffered from hunger. But the whole truth, even if Mayakovsky had been aware of it, was unprintable. The fact was that fewer than 40% of the workers were there voluntarily. Dispossessed peasants (or "special settlers," as they were called), forcibly removed from their villages during collectivization and simply dumped in Siberia with no provisions, made up the lion's share of the work force. Suffering from starvation, disease, and exhaustion, living in dugouts, contending with temperatures as low as -50 degrees C, they worked 12 hours a day and longer under the supervision of the local NKVD.(5) There was also prison la-

---

(4) "Komsomol'skoe znamya", Kiev, August 8, 1965 (as cited in Kovalenko, S. A. Kommentarii k stikhotvoreniyu V. V. Mayakovskogo, http://v-v-mayakovsky.ru/books/item/f00/s00/z0000006/st046.shtml, accessed Sept. 2017).

(5) Mark Ural'skii. "Kuznetskstroy: literaturnyy mif kak dokument epokhi," *Novii Zhurnal*, No. 287. http://magazines.russ.ru/nj/2017/287/kuzneckstroj-literaturnyj-mif-kak-dokument-epohi.html.

bor—the Siberian division of the Gulag (Siblag) was created in the fall of 1929, and by the spring of 1931 about 4,000 prisoners were working in the mines of the Kyznetsk Basin.[6]

Темно свинцовоночие/The rainclouds are dark as night
Literally, "the leaden night is dark." A play on the set phase "свинцовые тучи/leaden rain clouds."

лучину жгут/they light a *luchina*
A *luchina* is a large wooden splinter used in place of a candle, typically for lighting a peasant hut.

Сливеют губы/lips turn blue
A combo of "сливать/fuse together" and "синеть/turn blue."

Свела промозглость корчею/ Everyone is cramped in the soggy weather
Literally, "the dankness led to cramping." "Корчь/cramping" is formed from the verb "корчить/to cramp."

неважный мокр уют/Not much comfort in the wetness
Literally, "the poor comfort is wet."

встанутстройки стенами/buildings will rise up here in walls
A combination of "рядами/in rows" and "вставать стеной/to take a stand."

стоугольный «Гигант»/the super coal mine "the Giant"
Literally the "hundred-coal 'Giant,'" meaning that it would produce 100 times more coal than a normal mine. Construction on the first three major mines began in 1930, but it seems that none of these were actually nicknamed "the Giant."

ситный/sifted bread
Light fluffy bread with no clumps (or rocks, glass, or dirt).

над темью тучных стад/above masses of dark clouds
A clever play on words. The cliche "стада туч/flocks of clouds," becomes "тучные стада/fat flocks."

(6) Winston T. Bell. "The Gulag and Soviet Society in Western Siberia 1929-1953."PhD diss, University of Toronto, 2011.

Неокóнченное

I

Лю́бит? не лю́бит? Я рýки ломáю
и пáльцы
                разбрáсываю разломáвши
так рвут загадáв и пускáют
                                    по мáю
вéнчики встрéчных ромáшек
Пускáй седи́ны обнарýживает стри́жка и бритьё
Пусть серебрó годóв вызвáнивает
                                          ýймою
надéюсь вéрую вовéки не придёт
ко мне позóрное благоразýмие

II

Уже вторóй
                должнó быть ты леглá
А мóжет быть
                  и у тебя́ такóе
Я не спешý
                И мóлниями телегрáмм
мне нéзачем
                тебя́
                      буди́ть и беспокóить

III

мóре ухóдит вспять
мóре ухóдит спать
Как говоря́т инцидéнт испéрчен
любóвная лóдка разби́лась о быт
С тобóй мы в расчёте
И нé к чемý пéречень
взаи́мных бóлей бед и оби́д

Unfinished

I

She loves me? She loves me not? I'm wringing my hands
and scattering
                    broken fingers
the way you tell your fortune, pulling petals from wayside daisies
and releasing them
                              into May
Let a shave and haircut uncover grey hair
Let the silver of years ring out
                                             in masses
I hope I have faith that shameful good sense
will never come to me.

II

Already past one
                         you've probably gone to bed
But maybe
               you're in the same situation
I won't hurry
                    with lightning of telegrams
there's no point
                       in waking and bothering
                                                          you.

III

the sea goes away again
the sea goes away to sleep
As they say the incident is closed
love's boat has crashed on convention
You and I are even
and there's no point in listing
the mutual sufferings misfortunes and resentments

IV

Уже́ второ́й
должно́ быть ты легла́
В ночи́ Млечпу́ть сере́бряной Око́ю
Я не спешу́ и мо́лниями телегра́мм
Мне не́зачем тебя́ буди́ть и беспоко́ить
как говоря́т инциде́нт испе́рчен
любо́вная ло́дка разби́лась о быт
С тобо́й мы в расчёте и не́ к чему пе́речень
взаи́мных бо́лей бед и оби́д
Ты посмотри́ кака́я в ми́ре тишь
Ночь обложи́ла не́бо звёздной да́нью
в таки́е вот часы́ встаёшь и говори́шь
века́м исто́рии и мирозда́нию

V

Я зна́ю си́лу слов, я зна́ю слов наба́т.
Они́ не те, кото́рым рукопле́щут ло́жи.
От слов таки́х срыва́ются гроба́
шага́ть четвёркою свои́х дубо́вых но́жек.
Быва́ет, вы́бросят, не напеча́тав, не изда́в,
но сло́во мчи́тся, подтяну́в подпру́ги,
звени́т века́, и подполза́ют поезда́
лиза́ть поэ́зии мозо́листые ру́ки.
Я зна́ю си́лу слов. Гляди́тся пустяко́м,
опа́вшим лепестко́м под каблука́ми та́нца,
но челове́к душо́й губа́ми костяко́м

1930

IV

It's already past one you've probably gone to bed
In the night the Milkway is like the silver Oka
I won't rush and it's useless
to wake and disturb you with lightning of telegrams
As they say the incident is settled
love's boat has shattered on mundanity
You and I are even and there's no point in enumerating
the mutual sufferings misfortunes and resentments
Look how silent the earth is
Night has laid a starry yoke on the sky
In hours like these you stand and speak
to centuries to history and to the universe

V

I know the power of words I know the town bell of words
Not the ones that the box seats applaud
but the kind of words that make coffins break loose
and walk on their four oaken legs.
At times they'll be discarded, unprinted, unpublished,
but the word races along, tightening the saddle-girths,
rings for centuries, and trains crawl up
to lick poetry's calloused hands.
I know the power of words. It looks like a trifle,
a petal fallen under the heel of a dance,
but a man in his soul, his lips, his bones

Неоконченное/Unfinished

These are M's final poems, found among his notes after his suicide in April, 1930. In format, these are close to his earliest poems—for the most part the meter is regular (dactyls and iambs) and the layout is standard. But in tone these are far away from the poems of his youth. There's no "face punching," no self-aggrandizement, no wailing and gnashing of teeth. These are the poems of a mature artist—simple, quiet and incredibly poignant. (1)

I

Я руки ломаю/i wring my hands
A very strong expression of grief, literally "I'm breaking my arms."

по маю/into May
The usual expression is "по ветру/into the wind."

позорное благоразумие/shameful good sense
M's last lines are an echo of his first lines. From his 1912 debut in *A Slap in the Face of Public Taste*:

> And if FOR THE TIME BEING now the filthy brand of your "common sense" and "good taste" is yet present in our lines, they nevertheless – FOR THE FIRST TIME – already thrill with the Summer Lightning of the New Impending Beauty of the Self-valuable (self-creating) Word. (2)

IV

Млечпуть/Milkway
M has cut the ending off of the adjective "млечный/milky" and attached the root to the noun "путь/way." This is characteristic of the early vocabulary of Russian Soviet Republic, when hundreds of new words were created from abbreviations and acronyms.

---

(1) Bykov claims that "Море уходит вспять/Море уходит спать" are the best two lines from from M's late work—the culmination of his quest for a new style of honesty and absolute simplicity. 590.

(2) The translation is from *Volodya, Selected Works*, Carrick, 25.

серебряной Окою/a silver Oka

The Oka River, a tributary of the Volga, was the site of a famous battle between the Prince of Moscow and the Tartars, which signified the end of the "Mongol yoke," the Tartar-Mongol rule over the Slavs from the 13th through the 15th century.

молниями телеграмм

Телеграмма-молния, or "telegram-lightning" was an express telegram delivery service available in the '20s and '30s. Instead of treating the phrase as a unit, M has put the individual words in different cases. The normal declension would be "телеграммами-молниями," but here only "lightning" is instrumental; "telegrams" is genitive. "I won't rush . . . to wake you . . . with lightnings of telegrams."

звёздной данью/starry tribute

"Дань/tribute" is another word associated with Mongol rule. The phrase is also an echo of the poem's second line: "in the night . . . the silver Oka."

Как говорят, инцидент исперчен/As they say, the incident is over-peppered

A combination of "исчерпан/settled" and "испорчен/spoiled" which creates the word "исперчен/over-peppered."

As mentioned earlier, M used this stanza in his suicide note, but with two variations. In his note, the lines are in *lesenka* format, and the phrase "С тобой мы в расчёте/You and I are quits" is replaced with "Я с жизнью в расчёте/Life and I are quits."

V

Они не те, которым рукоплещут ложи/Not the ones applauded by the box seats

On January 21, 1930, M performed at the Bolshoi Theater to commemorate the 6th anniversary of Lenin's death. In the box seats sat Stalin and his entourage, and M's reading of "Vladimir Ilych Lenin" did indeed receive their sustained applause and approval. But this was an anomaly. By the time of this performance, M was at the edge of a precipice, deeply at odds with both the literary and political establishment. His play *The Bathhouse*, which debuted in January, was brutally criticized in the press; his retrospective *20 Years' Work*, which opened in February, was boycotted not only by party officials but by fellow authors; and the Soviet Encyclopedia, published in January 1930, stated that M was "opposed to the worldview of the proetariat," and that his "rebelliousness, anarchistic and individualistic, is essentially petit bourgeois."[(3)] Suicide is a persistent motif in M's work from his earliest poems,

(3) Jangfeldt, p. 495

and in 1930, at the age of 36, he had many justifications to end it all. He was no longer young ("You're old at thirty-five! I shall live till I'm thirty, no more."),[4] he was exhausted from his heavy schedule and frequent illnesses, his voice was failing, and he was at the painful end of yet another failed love affair.[5] But the decisive factor was his loss of faith in the revolution. Without communism, as he said, "love doesn't exist for me." But communism had been "beaten down by canaries"—the revolution had succumbed to petty bureaucrats, bosses and literary hacks. M was committed to "building a life," but there was no longer any material to work with, no ground left to stand on, and no power left to fight.

(4) Jangfeldt p. 564

(5) M's last love was the actress Nora Polonskaya, who refused his demands that she leave her husband. She was the last person to see him alive.

Bibliography

Almereyda, Michael, editor. *Night Wraps the Sky: Writings by and about Mayakovsky*. Farrar, Straus and Giroux, 2008.

Amelin, Gregory. *Lekcii po filosofii literatury.* Moscow, 2005.

Bell, Winston T. (2011). The Gulag and Soviet Society in Western Siberia 1929-1953 (Doctoral dissertation). Retreived from https://tspace.library.utoronto.ca/bitstream/1807/29921/1/Bell_Wilson_T_201106_PhD_thesis.pdf.

Bowlt, John E. "Natalia Goncharova and Futurist Theater." *Art Journal,* Vol. 49. Spring, 1990, pp. 44-51.

Boyn, Svetlana. *Common Places: Mythologies of Everyday Life*. Harvard University Press, 1995.

Brown, Edward J. *Mayakovsky: A Poet in the Revolution*. Princeton University Press, 1988.

Bykov, Dmitry. *Trinadcatii apostol. Mayakovskii: Tragediya-buff v shesti dejstviyah.* Young Guard, 2016.

Carrick, Rosy, editor. *Volodya: Selected Works*. Enitharmon Press, 2016.

Charters, Ann, and Samuel Charters. *I Love: The Story of Vladimir Mayakovsky and Lili Brik*. McGraw-Hill, 1979

Jangfeldt, Bengt, and Harry D. Watson. *Mayakovsky: a Biography*. The Univ. of Chicago Press, 2014.

Kovalenko, S. A. *Kommentarii k stikhotvoreniyu V. V. Mayakovskogo*. http://v-v-mayakovsky.ru/books/item/f00/s00/z0000006/st046.shtml.

Mayavkovsky, Vladimir. *Maloe sobranie sochinenii*. Alphabet, St. Petersburg, 2014.

Mayakovsky, Vladimir. *Polnoe sobranie sochineniy*. Maksim Moshkow and the Federal Agency of Print and Mass Communication. az.lib.ru/m/majakowskij_w_w.

Mayavkovsky, Vladimir and Neil Cornwell. *My Discovery of America*. Hesperus Press Limited, 2005.

Mayavkovsky, Vladimir and Guy Daniels. *Plays (European Drama Classics)* Northwestern University Press, 1995.

Mayavkovsky, Vladimir, and Gureyeva, Larisa et al. *Pro Eto - That's What.* Arc Publications, 2009.

Mayavkovsky, Vladimir and George Reavey. *"The Bedbug" and Selected Poetry*. Indiana University Press, 1985.

McGavran, James H, III. *Vladimir Mayakovsky Selected Poems*. Northwestern University Press, 2013.

Mikhaylov, Alexander. *Maiakovskii.* Moscow, 1988.

Muchnic, Helen. *From Gorky to Pasternak*. Vintage Books, 1961.

Smith, Gerard Stanton. *D.S. Mirsky: A Russian-English Life, 1890-1939.* Oxford University Press, 2000.

Troilet, Elsa, and Susan de Muth. *Mayakovsky: Russian Poet*. Hearing Eye, 2002.

Ural'skii, Mark. "Kuznetskstroy: literaturnyy mif kak dokument epokhi," *Novii Zhurnal*, No. 287. http://magazines.russ.ru/nj/2017/287/kuzneckstroj-literaturnyj-mif-kak-dokument-epohi.html.

Wachtel, Michael. *The Cambridge Introduction to Russian Poetry.* Cambridge University Press, 2004.

Wachtel, Michael. *The Development of Russian Verse.* Cambridge University Press, 1998.

Author's Biography

Jenny Wade is a musician (Swans, Timber, Rude Buddha, Vodka) and computer programmer who suffers from an obsession with 20th century Russian poetry. She has an MA in Russian Literature from UVA.

www.ingramcontent.com/pod-product-compliance
Lightning Source LLC
LaVergne TN
LVHW052335240826
846485LV00004B/47